The Black Death
The World's Most Devastating Plague

Dorsey Armstrong, Ph.D.

THE
GREAT
COURSES®

PUBLISHED BY:

THE GREAT COURSES
Corporate Headquarters
4840 Westfields Boulevard, Suite 500
Chantilly, Virginia 20151-2299
Phone: 1-800-832-2412
Fax: 703-378-3819
www.thegreatcourses.com

Dorsey Armstrong, Ph.D.
Professor of English
Purdue University

D r. Dorsey Armstrong is a Professor of English at Purdue University, where she has taught since 2002. She received her A.B. in English and Creative Writing from Stanford University and her Ph.D. in Medieval Literature from Duke University. She also has taught at Centenary College of Louisiana and at California State University, Long Beach.

Dr. Armstrong's research interests include medieval women writers, late-medieval print culture, and the Arthurian legend, on which she has published extensively. She is the author of *Sir Thomas Malory's* Morte Darthur: *A New Modern English Translation Based on the Winchester Manuscript* and *Gender and the Chivalric Community in Malory's* Morte d'Arthur. In January 2009, she became editor in chief of the academic journal *Arthuriana*, which publishes cutting-edge research on the legend of King Arthur, from its medieval origins to its modern enactments.

Dr. Armstrong's most recent book, *Mapping Malory: Regional Identities and National Geographies in* Le Morte Darthur (coauthored with Kenneth Hodges), is an exploration of the role played by geography in Malory's version of the story of King Arthur. Her current research project focuses on how medieval society reacted to and thought about twins and higher-order multiple births in literature and society.

Other Great Courses taught by Dr. Armstrong include *Turning Points in Medieval History*; *The Medieval World*; *Analysis and Critique: How to Engage and Write about Anything*; *Great Minds of the Medieval World*; and *King Arthur: History and Legend*. ■

Table of Contents

THE BLACK DEATH:
THE WORLD'S MOST DEVASTATING PLAGUE

SCOPE

In the mid-14th century, the medieval world experienced one of the most devastating pandemics to ever strike humankind: the Black Death. Between 1346 and 1353, this disease—commonly thought to be some form of bubonic plague—swept across Europe from the east in a clockwise motion, tightening around the medieval world like a noose. When it was finally over, at least half of the population was dead. Social structures, political and economic infrastructure, familial relationships, religious institutions, and more were all dramatically affected and, in many cases, irrevocably altered. Indeed, many scholars believe that it was the plague that served as the catalyst that began the process of transforming the medieval world into the modern one.

In this course, we'll explore the Black Death from multiple angles in order to understand how this pandemic originated, spread, and transformed the medieval world. Beginning with a discussion of what the medieval world looked like on the eve of the Black Death, we'll go on to examine plague's epidemiology and mode of transmission and then trace its progression across the 14th-century landscape. We'll see how plague was a key component of one of the first recorded instances of germ warfare, and how the city-states of Italy unwittingly facilitated plague's initial movement into the medieval world along its advanced and comprehensive trading networks. We'll examine first-person accounts from places like Florence, Sicily, Siena, Avignon, and more, in which the writers describe a landscape of death in once-bustling city centers: mass graves in public piazzas, a panicked mass exodus to the countryside, bodies lying in the streets or walled up in houses, and psychosocial responses that ranged from self-punishment to hedonistic orgies to pragmatic stoicism.

As we explore the plague's progression, we'll spend some time with some of the most recent theories about its source and transmission, including the recent discovery that gerbils—not rats—may have been one of the primary vectors of transmission. We'll also look at the range of arguments from many scholars that there was something besides bubonic plague raging through the medieval world at this time. A virulent strain of tuberculosis, anthrax exposure, an animal murrain that had leaped to humans, a heretofore unknown hemorrhagic fever similar to Ebola, and bacteria raining down from space: These and more are all explanations that have been put forward to explain why the mid-14th epidemic was so deadly.

As we track the plague's progress across the medieval world, we'll pause to perform "case studies" of individual communities who coped with the plague in unique ways. In Florence, we'll see how the government struggled to maintain normalcy and order in the face of utter devastation. In Avignon, we'll see how the seat of the papacy under Pope Clement VI attempted to cope with a threat not only to the population, but also to ecclesiastical authority. In Walsham, we'll see how a typical English village and manor estate was transformed when roughly 60–70 percent of the population died in the space of a few months.

We'll examine how the greatest medical and scientific minds of the day attempted to explain and cope with the Black Death, identifying planetary conjunctions, earthquakes, volcanic eruptions, and "bad air" or *miasma* as the cause of infection. We'll see how the Scandinavian countries and what is today Poland and Russia had a very different reaction to plague than did most of the rest of the medieval world, especially in terms of folklore and traditions in the countryside.

We'll meet the flagellants, who traveled from town to town and whipped themselves in public displays of fleshly humiliation, attempting by these means to appease God and obtain his mercy. We'll see how the Church's authority was radically undermined when members of the clergy died in record numbers and those who were left often refused to perform the duties of last rites or did so only reluctantly. While the institution of the Church suffered, popular religious practices were very much in evidence, as there was an increase in the practice of pilgrimage to holy sites. New "plague saints" became the recipients of prayers from an increasingly desperate population.

In this course, we'll also examine the few exceptions to the rule—communities that were somehow spared during the initial outbreak. Milan was saved by the policies of its draconian ruler, Nuremberg by its unusually advanced systems of sanitation and culture of hygiene, and Iceland by luck and timing.

After the initial discombobulation caused by the outbreak of plague, medieval society attempted to get back to normal—but it was a new normal, one that was constantly disrupted by continued outbreaks of plague every generation or so.

In response to the Black Death, new art forms and literature came into existence. Indeed, the careers of writers like Geoffrey Chaucer may have been made possible by the arrival of plague and the possibility for social mobility that came with it.

In the end, the medieval world was utterly transformed. For most of those who survived the plague, life was much better than it had been before. Religious institutions, economic practices, social and political infrastructure, and more were radically reshaped by the plague. From the ashes of the Black Death, a new world—and the Renaissance—was born. ∎

EUROPE ON THE BRINK OF THE BLACK DEATH

The Black Death, which raged through Europe in the 14th century, changed just about every single thing about medieval society. In large measure, it produced the modern world we live in today. This lecture starts by clearing up two common misconceptions about the Black Death. Then it moves on to describe in general terms how 14th-century European society functioned. Finally, the lecture discusses how that society was beginning to change, and gives a peek at how the Black Death sped those changes along.

TWO COMMON MISCONCEPTIONS

- To start off, let's deal with two common misconceptions. First of all, this disease is not called the Black Death because parts of the bodies of people who were infected turned black. The plague was often called the *bubonic plague* because in one form it produced large lumps—or buboes—around the lymph nodes, often at the armpit or groin. People seem to have assumed that the term Black Death refers to the color of those buboes.

- Rather, the term Black Death is used to suggest the horror of the epidemic, not the color of its symptoms. It was a dark, black, terrifying time.

- This leads to another misconception. No one in the Middle Ages called it the Black Death. It was the Great Mortality, or the Great Pestilence, or even, in some cases in England, blue sickness, but it was not called the Black Death until centuries after it initially spread through Europe, and later historians looked back and tried to write about it.

EUROPE AT THE TIME

- Let's try to get a snapshot of medieval Europe in the early 14th century, around 1340. Most of Europe in the Middle Ages was Christian, agrarian, and feudal. Let's take those terms in order.

- *Christian*: In the Middle Ages, there was no such thing as separation of Church and state. The Church owned more property than any other entity; the Church was deeply intertwined with education at every level, especially at the universities; the Church had many business, production, and trade interests; and the Church was deeply engaged and concerned with the politics of the day.

- *Agrarian*: Before the Middle Ages, there was the Roman Empire. Before it definitively ceased to exist in the 5th century, Rome had been a society that had both busy urban centers and farmland that fed its citizens. As Rome started to transform into the entities that we think of today as the countries of Western Europe, urban centers went into serious decline, and the majority of the population turned to farming—in many cases, subsistence farming—as the dominant way of life.

- *Feudal*: To explain what *feudal* means, let's examine a hypothetical king. He gets to stay king by offering his support and protection to the nobles just below him in the social order. In return for the right to be granted lands and titles, the nobles (or king's *vassals*) pledge their loyalty to the king.
  - Those nobles have lower-ranking men who pledge the same thing to them. This goes on down the line until we get to the peasants. Peasants have the right to work land and keep a portion of the crops they harvest as long as they give an agreed-upon amount of the harvest or a certain number of days of labor to their lord.

- In a feudal society, everybody is thus connected to everybody else along the lines of a pyramid structure.

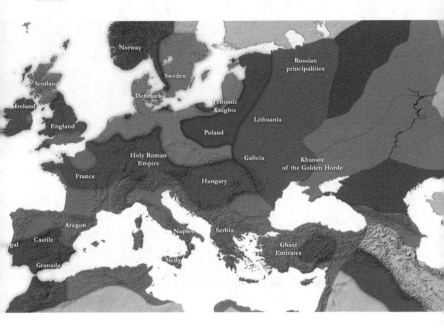

THE THREE ESTATES

- Medieval society was organized in terms of an idea known as the *three estates model*. According to this long-entrenched philosophy, people were born into one of three social orders—those who fight, those who pray, and those who work.

    - Those who fight, the nobles, were supposed to provide the protection to the rest of the social order.

    - Those who pray—the clergy, priests, monks, nuns, and so on—were supposed to be busying themselves with helping to save humanity from sin.

    - Those first two orders were supposed to be supported by the labor of those who work, the peasants. Peasants enjoyed the protection of the nobles in the earthly life and the prayers of the clergy to help them in the life to come.

- One was not supposed to aspire to move out of one's order. The idea was that people belong to the order to which they were born, and if society was going to function properly, then there was to be no moving outside one's estate.

- Members of the second estate, those who pray, typically got there by being born into the first estate as a second son or younger daughter. By the 14th century, most nobles and high-ranking landholders had figured out that the only way to maintain family heritage and power was to practice primogeniture, in which the eldest son inherits everything.

- Dividing lands and titles equally among heirs usually meant that within a generation or two, there'd be many cousins, each clinging desperately to a tiny parcel of land, fighting among themselves for position. No one would really have anything worth fighting over. Second and third sons, and younger daughters for whom there was no money or goods suitable for a dowry, would become monks or nuns and live out their lives in what could be quite comfortable and somewhat worldly religious houses.

- Percentage-wise, the population distribution was something like 5 percent first estate, 5 percent second estate, and 90 percent third estate. This means the majority of the members of medieval society were those who worked at the bottom to allow the top 10 percent to live off the fruits of their labor.

- In terms of literacy, this means that the few people who could read, and the fewer who could read *and* write, were mostly concentrated in that 10 percent at the top of the social order.

CHANGES

- The medieval model of society had begun to change a little by 1340, for a few reasons. One was the rise of a merchant class, which was able to develop in part because of a population boom that occurred between 1000 and 1300.

- Over the course of those three centuries, the population of Europe doubled from about 75 million people to around 150 million. This was due to a few influences, one of which was a period of global warming—called the *Little Climatic Optimum*, the *Medieval Warm Period*, or the *Medieval Climate*

Optimum—that increased the growing season. Another influence was advances in agricultural practice.

- The population boom created a sudden land crunch. With the practical doubling of the population in just three centuries, pretty much all arable land that could be worked was brought under the plow.

- With this land crunch, many people found themselves driven to the cities to find a way to make a living. This created, for the first time since the fall of the Roman Empire, urbanization on a significant scale in places like London, Paris, Rome, Florence, and Milan.

- An increase in trade and the movement of goods to and from far-flung locales served to create a new class that didn't quite fit into the three estates model. While the merchant class should technically belong to the 90 percent of "those who work," the members of that class started to look a little more like the top 5 percent, the nobles, or "those who fight." A shrewd businessman could make enough money to afford expensive clothes and education for his family.

THE BROAD PICTURE

- This pressure didn't present a real crisis to the social order—yet. Many historians, such as the great David Herlihy, have argued that without some sort of external factor coming into play, society in the Western world would have continued on more or less like this for a few more centuries. What we think of as the modern world—with its enlightenments and scientific discoveries and literary and artistic renaissances—would have been much longer in coming.

- In other words, as horrible as the Black Death was for those who lived through it, the world that rose from its ashes was a better world with more possibilities for those who had survived its horrors. For one thing, the rigid boundaries of the three estates ideal would be blown to absolute smithereens in the aftermath of the plague.

- It seems an interesting little twist of history that the plague, in the opinion of most historians, moved westward along trade routes. Those merchants and tradesmen who had been so eager to move goods along these routes were the ones whose families benefited in the long term once the ravages of plague had abated.

- With up to half the population dead, the great nobles didn't have enough laborers to work their lands. The peasants who had been tied to a particular land or manor found that they could walk down the road and offer their services to another nobleman who might, in his desperation to get the harvest in, be willing to pay a large cash wage.

- The nobles, rich in titles and land holdings but cash poor, started to marry into the merchant class; the merchants in turn were delighted to see their sons and daughters work their way up the social hierarchy. Indeed, the great author Geoffrey Chaucer's granddaughter, Alice de la Pole, became the duchess of Suffolk. When the first wave of plague had passed, it was a brave new world that emerged. The medieval world in 1340 and the medieval world in 1360 were two very different places.

QUESTIONS TO CONSIDER

1. What are the main ways in which the medieval world differs from our modern one? Where do you see similarities?

2. What is the most surprising thing to you about the structure of medieval life?

SUGGESTED READING

Gies and Gies, *Daily Life in Medieval Times.*

Rosenwein, *A Short History of the Middle Ages.*

THE EPIDEMIOLOGY OF PLAGUE

I n Europe, for about a decade in the middle of the 14th century, it must have seemed like the world was coming to an end. The Black Death made its way westward, killing a third to a half of the population of the medieval world. The disease exhibited a confusing variety of permutations. This lecture identifies and describes the three forms the plague took. Then it looks at a disturbing reality: The plague didn't happen only in the 14th century.

OTHER PLAGUES

- The Black Death of the 14th century was such a traumatic event that it's difficult to imagine there could ever have been anything like it before, or that anything like it could happen again. But massive plagues did occur before and after. In the 6th century, the so-called Plague of Justinian had contributed to the final disintegration of what was left of the Western Roman Empire.

- In the 19th century in Asia, plague would once again cause death, suffering, and panic. It is the 19th-century plague—and modern medicine's attempts to understand it—that would ultimately offer us some answers about the Black Death and the earlier plague in 6th century.

- In order to understand the epidemiology of plague and how it impacted the medieval world, let's start by examining what scientists were able to figure out by studying the disease in the modern era. The year is 1894, and the place is Canton, China. Starting a few years earlier, there had been outbreaks of plague in Yunnan province and in India.

- While these outbreaks were not as severe as either the 6th-century Plague of Justinian or the 14th-century Black Death, they were still scary—estimates suggest that somewhere between 50,000 to 125,000 people were infected and 80 percent of those who contracted plague would die from it.

- Two scientists working in Hong Kong—a Japanese student of Robert Koch named Shibasaburo Kitasato and a Swiss-French student of Louis Pasteur's named Alexandre Yersin—almost simultaneously managed to isolate the cause of plague in the laboratory after careful examination of tissue samples of those infected.

- Kitasato was a little quicker in discovering the source of plague, but Yersin's description of the bacterium was more thorough and accurate. From 1894 on, the bacterium that causes plague has been called *Yersinia pestis* in Yersin's honor.

- A few years after isolating and identifying the bacillus, Yersin identified rats as the prime carrier of the disease. In 1898, a scientist named Paul-Louis Simond argued conclusively that the disease is transmitted to humans when fleas jump from a rat to a human being and bite that human being. What this means is that plague is *zoonotic*: Like smallpox and some other diseases, it originates in animals, and then jumps from animals and infects the human population.

How Transmission Works

- Many kinds of rodents can carry plague. Fleas that feed on rats, guinea pigs, and other similar animals, like squirrels, can become infected with plague. But just because a flea is infected doesn't mean that it's infective.

- The way that fleas become infective is due to a feature of their alimentary system—they have not only a stomach, or a ventriculus, but also a proventriculus, which acts as a valve that regulates the food that the flea is ingesting and trying to get to its stomach.

- When a flea feeds on a plague-infected rodent, the nourishment doesn't pass to the ventriculus as quickly or as easily as it would if a flea were feeding on a non-infected rodent. A blockage of bacteria and blood forms in the proventriculus, so that nourishment can't get to the flea's stomach.

- Now the very hungry flea starts biting more aggressively and frequently in order to get some nourishment, yet the blockage in the proventriculus just gets bigger and bigger. Finally, the flea's system realizes what's happening, and regurgitates the blockage out of the proventriculus.

- The regurgitated matter goes directly into the system of whatever the flea is feeding on. If it's a human being, and the flea has jumped there from a black rat, then the starving flea will aggressively regurgitate, feed, and repeat.

- Studies conducted in the 1970s suggested that it was crucial that the biting flea be a rat flea, and also that the fleas typically found on humans don't really transmit plague—the proportion of plague in the blood of an infected human didn't seem to be enough to cause a blockage in the digestive system of fleas that are usually found on people. So, the theory went, you had to have rats as hosts, and then those hosts needed to die, so the rat flea was forced to find a food source that it would not typically have chosen—in this case, humans.

- Although the same bacillus seems to have been primarily responsible for the three plagues—of the late antique world, the medieval era, and the modern period—their epidemiology and etiology seem to differ a bit, suggesting that the bacterium itself has undergone some evolutionary shifts at different times in its existence.

THE BUBONIC FORM

- Let's say an infected and infective rat flea has bitten you. What happens next? In most people, large swollen areas develop around the lymph nodes, usually at the neck, groin, and armpits. These lumps are called *buboes*, and it is from this word that we get the most common name we use for the Black Death—the bubonic plague.

- If you get the bubonic form of the plague, you have around an 18 percent chance of surviving. With the bubonic form, human-to-human transmission seems to be almost impossible, although it may have occurred in some instances when doctors or caretakers tried to effect a cure by lancing the buboes.

- First-person accounts of this process from the period indicate that the pus that came out when this operation was performed was disgusting not only in appearance but also in terms of the smell. A few accounts relate that the doctor and others in the room were so overcome by the stench that they often vomited or fainted. But again, this seems to be the form of plague that a person just might survive.

THE PNEUMONIC FORM

- Pneumonic plague was the second most common form of plague. In this case *Yersinia pestis* has set up shop in the sufferer's respiratory system, rather than in the lymphatic system, as is the case with the bubonic form. It starts, usually, with a patient zero who has been infected with the bubonic form of the disease, which then makes its way from her lymphatic system into her respiratory system.

- This form of plague is easily transmissible from person to person. A doctor or friend or relative taking care of someone infected with the pneumonic form of the plague is going to come in contact with blood, sputum, or saliva containing the bacterium, and will usually themselves become infected—unless someone is alert enough to recognize this for what it is and put on a hazmat suit. Modern hazmat suits, of course, weren't available in the Middle Ages.

- The way a person died was usually from drowning in their own blood. The good news: The time from onset of symptoms to death is usually just two days. The bad news: The suffering is intense and the survival rate is less than 1 percent.

THE SEPTICEMIC FORM

- The third and least common form of plague is the septicemic form, which is an infection of the blood. Like pneumonic plague, this form can

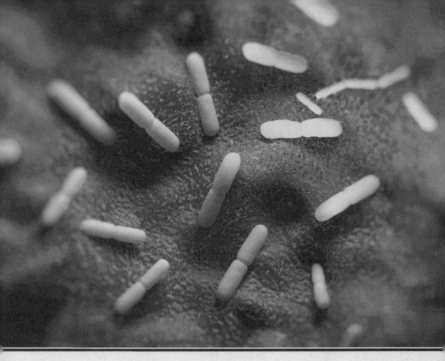

start out as bubonic. Then the infection can move to a different bodily system.

- When plague bacteria enter the bloodstream, they cause something known as *disseminated intravascular coagulation*, or DIC. In these instances, tiny blood clots start to form throughout the body, which results in something called *localized ischemic necrosis*, which means portions of body tissue start to die off due to lack of circulation.

- If you have septicemic plague, and it's pretty well advanced, your blood starts to lose the ability to clot properly. If your blood doesn't clot, it starts to seep into other parts of your body, like your skin and internal organs.

- This produces red and black patchy rashes and bumps on the skin that look rather like pimples all over your body. Most scholars think that these visible indicators are what medieval people meant when they said that a dead person bore "the sign" of the plague. A final common sign of advanced septicemic plague is the vomiting of blood. Death could occur within 24 hours of symptoms showing.

LATER PLAGUE

- Although we began this lecture talking about the three major outbreaks of plague—in the 6th, the 14th, and the 19th centuries—it's not that plague completely disappeared in between. Indeed, it periodically flared up again after the initial waves of infection and, in the case of the Black Death of the Middle Ages, kept reappearing, in milder forms, with some regularity in Europe until about the 17th century.

- While the basic epidemiology seemed to be the same in subsequent outbreaks, the nature of plague did seem to shift or evolve. For example, in England toward the end of the 14th century, there was a wave of plague that seemed to target only the healthiest people.

- Plague still exists today. In 2015 there were at least 15 cases, usually due to people coming into contact with plague-infected rodents in mountain or wilderness areas. If the doctors can figure out what it is quickly enough, the plague can usually be easily cured with a course of antibiotics—usually streptomycin or gentamicin, although a few others are sometimes used. Unfortunately, because plague is so rare these days, doctors don't always recognize it when it appears, and there have been some deaths from plague in the U.S. in the last several decades.

- Scholars seem pretty certain that the two earlier, devastating outbreaks of disease in the Western world are a pretty good match for the epidemic that occurred in 1894 in Asia. For example, let's look quickly at the Plague of Justinian.

- Contemporary accounts suggest that the disease originated in China and then moved with rats along trade routes to Egypt and Constantinople. The plague first appeared around 541, and is called the Plague of Justinian because the emperor himself contracted the plague but was lucky enough to survive.

- Especially hard hit during this outbreak was the city of Constantinople, capital of what had been the eastern half of the Roman Empire, and which at this point was well into its transformation into the Byzantine Empire. The historian and scholar Procopius wrote that in that city, up to 10,000 people a day were dying, and the bodies were stacked up in the streets because there was no place to put them. It's hard to gauge the accuracy of these accounts, but scholars guess that the plague may have claimed up to 40 percent of the population.

- Justinian's attempts to reunite the Roman Empire crumbled in the wake of the plague's devastation, as there were not enough able-bodied men to serve in the military, and not enough active farmland to be taxed to pay those military forces. For the next two centuries, the plague would make periodic reappearances, landing blow after blow to the social infrastructure at precisely the moments it seemed to be recovering.

QUESTIONS TO CONSIDER

1. Apart from using antibiotics on those already infected, what would seem to be the best way to prevent future outbreaks of plague in the modern world?

2. Is there anything that medieval people could have done—given their limited understanding of germs, bacteria, etc.—that might have mitigated the transmission of plague?

SUGGESTED READING

Benedictow, *The Black Death 1346–1353*.

Slack, *Plague: A Very Short Introduction*.

DID PLAGUE REALLY CAUSE THE BLACK DEATH?

I
n recent years, many scholars have suggested that while plague may be partially responsible for the high mortality rates in the middle of the 14th century, the virulence and speed with which death swept through Western Europe doesn't completely make sense if we assign *only* plague as its primary cause. This lecture starts out by looking at some factors that complicate the candidacy of plague as the sole 14th-century mass killer. Then it moves on to examine some alternate theories, which have varying degrees of plausibility.

COMPLICATIONS

- Scientists have discovered that about 10–20 percent of the population of Western Europe has a natural immunity to HIV/AIDS, and that the mutation accounting for this seems to be connected to having an ancestor who survived the plague. At first, this doesn't make any sense at all, as the plague is bacterial and HIV/AIDS is viral—unless what was sweeping across the continent was not only bubonic plague, but also some kind of hemorrhagic fever.

- One of the first medieval scholars to aggressively question the causes of the Black Death and raise questions about its impact was the late historian David Herlihy, a specialist who worked extensively on medieval Italy.

- Herlihy noted that almost nowhere in the accounts of medieval plague's advance does anyone mention an epizootic event. This would be a massive die-off of the rats who are the black fleas' primary host, causing the fleas to jump to humans. In the case of the 19th-century plague in India and China, several accounts attest to this die-off as preceding the onslaught of plague.

- Herlihy also was one of the first to raise the point that the speed with which plague swept through the medieval world isn't satisfactorily explained by the argument that the Black Death moved along trade routes. With the exception of pneumonic plague, humans can't infect other humans, so a very large number of infected rats and their fleas would have to have hitched rides westward in caravans and onboard ships.

- Also, plague seemed to move in seasonal cycles—getting worse in the summer, disappearing for a time in the winter, and then usually reappearing again when the weather turned warm. Epidemiologically, it would make more sense for winter to be the worst time of infection— everyone is indoors, humans and rats side by side, increasing the chances of plague transmission. But that's not what tended to happen.

- There are other factors complicating the argument that what struck the medieval world in the 14th century was only bubonic plague. For example, in Florence, Italy, starting in 1377—after the first big wave of plague had ravaged the region—those who were responsible for preparing bodies for burial would note in the *Libri dei Morti*—or "Books of the Dead"—what had been the cause of death, when it could be determined.

- By 1424, if someone had died of plague, there would be a notation that read *de segno*, or "with the sign," meaning "the sign of the plague." For good measure, there would often be a big P added as well. All the evidence suggests that people considered these later epidemics recurrences of what had happened in 1348, and not a new disease.

- The sign was so well known that not many scribes bother to tell us what the sign is. In Viterbo, Italy, there are mentions in the surviving documents of *lenticulae* or *petechiae* or marks on the body that look something like freckles. In medieval England, we hear references to the "Blue Sickness," which seems to indicate that sufferers of the epidemic would develop bruised-looking patches on their skin. What's noteworthy here is that many of these descriptions don't mention buboes at all, or do so only occasionally.

ANTHRAX

- In 1984, an epidemiologist named Graham Twigg published what was, at the time, considered a radical rethinking of the causes of the Black Death. He argued that most of the medieval epidemics were not the plague at all but, in fact, were caused by exposure to anthrax. Anthrax is a bacillus—like *Yersinia pestis*—and it is found to be naturally occurring on every continent.

- Infection usually occurs when grazing animals inhale the *Bacillus anthracis* spores; the infection jumps to humans if we consume meat from infected animals. You can also contract anthrax if you come into contact with the

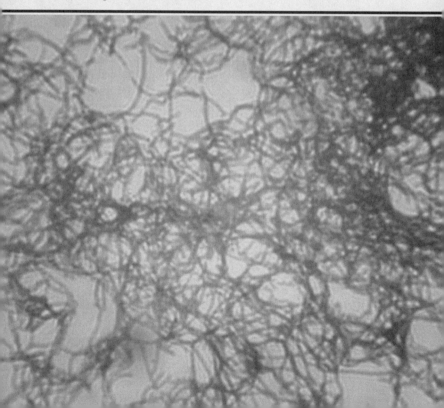

Microscopic image of Bacillus anthracis

clothing or shoes of someone who has encountered anthrax spores out in nature.

- It's the hardiness of the anthrax spores that has attracted modern interest in them as biological weapons. In fact, live anthrax spores have been discovered in the soil covering an animal that died of that disease 70 years earlier.

- In the mid-19th century Louis Pasteur came up with a vaccine for anthrax; prior to that it was a regular occurrence for thousands of animals and humans to die from anthrax every year. While anthrax is considered to be under control in most of the developed world, infection still does occur to this day in parts of the globe that don't have much in the way of a veterinary infrastructure.

- If you inhale anthrax spores, you usually have some flulike symptoms for a few days, then severe pneumonia and respiratory collapse—symptoms that sound an awful like the pneumonic form of plague. And if you eat infected meat, you have serious gastrointestinal issues and end up vomiting blood, which sounds a lot like the symptoms sometimes associated with all three forms of plague. Even more to the point: Boils and lesions often show up on the bodies of those infected.

- Historically, it's estimated that fatality rates for anthrax were around 85 percent; in the modern period, if anthrax is diagnosed and treated quickly, the fatality rate is closer to 45 percent. Again, that sounds a lot like plague.

- Historian Norman Cantor points out that anthrax spores have been found in a plague pit—or mass grave—dating from the Middle Ages in Scotland, and there is evidence that meat from slaughtered murrain-infected cattle was sold in villages in England shortly before the first big outbreak there in 1348. (*Murrain* was originally a medieval word that at first just meant "death," but which underwent linguistic specialization and came to mean any disease that affected cattle and sheep.)

- There are some scholars who have more cautiously proposed that while anthrax may be the cause, it would be safer and more correct to argue that some sort of cattle and/or sheep murrain may have been a contributor.

SPACE

- One of the most interesting theories about plague is that it comes from space. This theory was first proposed in 1979 by Fred Hoyle, an astrophysicist who had had a long career at Cambridge University, and Nalin Chandra Wickramasinghe in their coauthored book, *Diseases from Space*.

- Their theory rests on something called *panspermia*, which is the idea that the seeds of life exist all through the universe, and those seeds move through the galaxies as part of comets, asteroids, and other such bodies. When those bodies crash into a planet like ours—sometimes carrying with them bacteria that can cause disease—we have what Hoyle and Wickramasinghe call *vertical transmission*.

- Hoyle and Wickramasinghe argue that bubonic plague seems to be a likely candidate for a disease that was vertically transmitted from space. They claim that this explains why plague appeared in the 6th century, then again in the 14th, and then again in the 19th, with such long gaps in between outbreaks. Where was *Yersinia pestis* hiding all this time? Their answer is: not on Earth.

- Indeed, while the authors acknowledge the role that the black rat played in the outbreak of the Black Death, they also are quick to point out the flaws in the theory that these rodents were the main means of transmission: "There was no marching army of plague stricken rats. The rats died in the places where they were."

- Dr. Chris Patil, a biologist who also is one of the select 100 people who are currently training for the Mars One program, says he might cautiously agree that the idea that life on Earth—at least some of it—may have originated elsewhere has some points in its favor. But at the same time, the specifics of Hoyle and Wickramasinghe's theory is considered very fringe by the scientific community at large, and pretty much every mainstream scientist feels that the theory doesn't really hold water, and certainly can't be proved.

REASONS FOR DOUBT

- There is good reason for there to be such doubt surrounding the theory that *Yersinia pestis* is the prime cause of the Black Death, however. One point that scholars and scientists return to again and again, as you've seen, is the problem of the means of transmission. The black rat did not suddenly decide to migrate west, then south, then northwest, and back east again all of a sudden starting in 1346.

- There also doesn't seem to be a logical correlation between outbreaks and the seasons. For example, some of the worst outbreaks occurred during really hot Mediterranean summers in Italy—but that's exactly when rat fleas were least likely to be thriving. Plague also was reported to have occurred in Scandinavia in the dead of winter.

- In early 2015, a study came out of the University of Oslo suggesting that black rats—or any rats—may not have been responsible at all. The study—published in the *Proceedings of the National Academy of Sciences*—demonstrated that plague outbreaks in Europe don't correspond to weather in Europe. The outbreaks seem to have a correlation to weather in Asia, particularly to years when there were wet springs and warm summers.

- Most scholars agree that the outbreak seems to have originated in Asia and then moved west along trade routes. But these weather patterns are not conducive to breeding black rats. Therefore, the dominant theory seems to not quite fit—unless you turn to another rodent that carries fleas. And that rodent, the authors argue, was the gerbil.

- The authors of the study say that when there was spate of weather that provided an ideal breeding climate for gerbils—and of course, their fleas—this period was predictably followed by outbreaks of plague moving west. Again, there seem to be more than a few possible holes in this theory, but no one theory we've examined adequately explains how and why the plague showed up when it did, moved as quickly as it did, killed as many people as it did, and then disappeared for so long.

- Many people have pointed out that for as deadly as the plague was in the 14th century, it seemed rather a weak shadow of the Black Death when it appeared in the late 19th century. To explain this, some scientists have proposed that the modern plague was caused by an evolutionarily much weaker form of *Yersinia pestis*. This would make sense, because the medieval form of plague was so virulent, it would seem that unless it evolved into a less deadly form, it was at risk of wiping itself out by killing all its potential hosts.

- In a series of articles that have been appearing since about 2000, several different scientists have written reports about what they've discovered using DNA analysis of corpses excavated from plague cemeteries. A study published by the journal *PLOS Pathogens* in 2010 found specific DNA and protein signatures in a variety of skeletons from throughout northern, central, and southern Europe, and also identified two previously unknown genetic branches of *Yersinia pestis* that were associated with specific mass graves. This suggests that the plague came into Europe in two distinct waves. These two variants now appear to be extinct.

QUESTIONS TO CONSIDER

1. Which alternate plague theory seems most likely / possible to you?

2. How might understanding that multiple diseases were possibly in play in the Middle Ages help us confront modern diseases today?

SUGGESTED READING

Byrne, *The Black Death.*

Herlihy, *The Black Death and the Transformation of the West.*

THE BLACK DEATH'S PORTS OF ENTRY

The most likely cause of the bubonic plague, the *Yersinia pestis* bacterium, started in Asia and then made its way west, south, and northwest. It then looped around back east, tightening around the medieval European world like a noose. So how exactly did the plague move from Asia into Europe? Well, we can answer that question in a general sense—it came along the trade routes. But in this lecture, we're going to get more specific: How did it initially make contact with the European world? Using the first-person accounts of medieval people and some modern-day detective work, we'll get pretty close to having an answer.

TRADE AND PLAGUE

- When it comes to trade in medieval Europe, one group of people stands out: the Italians. The Italian Peninsula, in its prime position extending down into the Mediterranean and connected to the European landmass, had been a center of trade for centuries, and Italian merchants and sailors had gotten pretty good at moving goods and services among Africa, Asia, the Middle East, and Western Europe.

- It's important to clarify that it's not really correct to refer to these peoples as "Italians." Italy was far from unified at this point in time, and in effect it was a collection of city-states. Florentines considered themselves different from Venetians, who were definitely different from Neapolitans, who were not the same as the Milanese. Sicilians were another group at an even further remove.

- In the year 1266, a group of Genoese traders and merchants established a center of trade at a place called Caffa, which today is called Feodosia. This port city is on the Crimean Peninsula, on the Black Sea. In order to set up a trading center there, the Genoese had to enter into an agreement with the ruling people of that area: the Tatars, also called the Mongols or the Golden Horde.

- From the Italian Peninsula, Genoese and other merchants could move from the Mediterranean into the Aegean Sea, and from there through the Dardanelles into the Sea of Marmara, then through the Bosporus into the Black Sea, where they could put in at Caffa.

- From there, they could move into the Sea of Azov. The Genoese had established an outpost in the northeast corner of the Sea of Azov, at a place that was then called Tana. From Tana, they could extend their trade route both overland into the Middle East and along the Don River into Russia.

- In 1343, there was what amounts to a street fight between some of the Italian population of Tana and some of the Muslim population. The forces of the Mongol leader, Jani Beg, tried to arrest the Genoese who were involved. They, in turn, hopped in their boats and fled south and west across the Sea of Azov, into the Black Sea, and took refuge in Caffa.

- Jani Beg decided to attack the city, and he laid siege to it off and on for two years. This situation might have continued pretty much indefinitely were it not for something totally unexpected: In 1345, Jani Beg's forces were ravaged by plague, which had started to make its way west.

FIRST CONTACT

- The Mongol forces recognized that they were defeated and that the siege was over, but before they withdrew, they engaged in what microbiologist Mark Wheelis has described as "the most spectacular incident of biological warfare ever." They loaded up their trebuchets with plague corpses and launched them into the city.

- It is this event that many contemporary chroniclers identified as the "first contact" between the European world and the plague. This belief that informs the first-person account of Gabriele de' Mussi, who wrote one of the first accounts of the plague's arrival in Europe. He wrote in Latin, in a text that has come to be called the *Historia de Morbo*.

- Here, in Rosemary Horrox's excellent translation from the Latin, is a key passage, to which historians, scientists, medical professionals, and literary scholars alike have turned over the years in an attempt to understand the nature of the plague:

    > Oh God! See how the heathen Tartar races, pouring together from all sides, suddenly infested the city of Caffa and besieged the trapped Christians there for almost three years. ... But behold, the whole army was affected by a disease which overran the Tartars and killed thousands upon thousands every day. ... All medical advice and attention was useless; the Tartars died as soon as the signs of disease appeared on their bodies: swellings in the armpit or groin caused by coagulating humors, followed by a putrid fever.

- Interesting to scholars is the very specific reference to buboes appearing in those infected. This seems pretty clearly to be a case of bubonic plague.

- De' Mussi goes on to recount "mountains of dead" and "thousands of corpses," which may be more or less correct, given what we can surmise about the size of Jani Beg's army and the mortality rates associated with plague.

- Even if there were no fleas on these corpses—and there likely were on many—most of the bodies probably had open wounds, either from warfare or from attempts to lance the buboes. Those in the city may also have had open wounds—certainly, there would be cuts and scrapes, especially if there was a need for a large contingent of people to drag catapulted corpses to the sea and try to dispose of them. This open-wound contact may indeed have caused infection in Caffa.

- De' Mussi goes on to give several poignant descriptions of what life has been like in the city up to the time of his account:
    - Mass graves dug in colonnades and piazzas.

- Sick people abandoned by terrified family members.
- Priests afraid to administer last rites.
- Healthy people recognizing there was no defense and planning for their own deaths.
- Renewed turn to faith and prayers offered to particular intercessory saints, many of whom had languished in obscurity for some time but who were now very much in vogue.

OTHER ROUTES

- The Italian Peninsula was ground zero for infection, but the plague entered Europe through a variety of routes. In 1346, plague activity was happening to the northwest of the Caspian Sea and the northeast of the Black Sea and the Sea of Azov. It struck Caffa, and then in 1347, the area around Constantinople was hit particularly hard.

- As Constantinople was a major center for trade, it's very likely traders were unwittingly bringing plague with them, whichever direction they were heading. Sailors and merchants—primarily from the Italian Peninsula—brought it into the European world.

- The plague struck port cities first, and then these pockets of infection spread to the rest of the continent. In 1347 it shows up on Crete, on Cyprus, in southern Greece, and in Alexandria in Egypt.

- A look at the map of Italy and modern-day Croatia reveals even more emphatically the multiple points of entry for plague into the medieval European world: Dubrovnik, Split, Venice, Sicily, Pisa, and Genoa all were infected in 1347, as were Marseille, Aix-en-Provence, Avignon in France, and Mallorca off the coast of Spain. In 1348, the plague then spread inland from these initial entry points, and the rest, as they say, is history.

- A logical question to ask is: How could an infected ship's crew survive such a long journey from Caffa all the way to Genoa without everybody succumbing to the plague? Our best guess here is that the ships in question had a large and diverse group of people on board. The numbers must have been high enough that the infection couldn't make its way through everyone all that quickly. Additionally, with the bubonic form of plague, there could have been survival rates around 18–20%.

- The distance from Genoa to Caffa is 2,160 nautical miles. If we assume a conservative speed of five knots, then it would take about 18 days to make the trip between the two. The trip from plague-infested Constantinople would have taken even less time—under two weeks in good conditions.

- Therefore, the plague may not have had enough time to fully work its way through the crew of a ship. Some sailors indeed may have been just starting to show signs of illness when they made landfall, prompting them to seek out treatment and hospitality from the closest friend or acquaintance they could find.

VILLANI

- As the plague made its first significant European incursion into Italy, it's no surprise that it was Italian writers, like Gabriele de' Mussi, who were the first to chronicle its progression.

- A middle-class Florentine named Giovanni Villani discussed the Black Death's appearance in his history in a work called the *Nuova Cronica*. Villani was already writing a history when the Black Death began to sweep across the Italian Peninsula, and he included this in his account of the progression of historical events.

- Villani was inspired to write a history of Florence on the occasion of the jubilee in Rome in the year 1300, on which occasion Pope Boniface VIII issued a huge number of papal indulgences in honor of Christ's nativity. Villani relates that on this occasion, it occurred to him that Rome seemed to be in decline, while the fortunes of Florence were rising.

- In late 1347 and early 1348, he turned his attention to the Black Death, which had appeared in Italy's major port cities around September and

GIOVANNI VILLANI

October of 1347, and which was in full force by December. His chronicle ends with the following paragraph:

> Having grown in vigor in Turkey and Greece and having spread thence over the whole Levant and Mesopotamia and Syria and Chaldea and Cyprus and Rhodes and all the islands of the Greek archipelago, the said pestilence leaped to Sicily, Sardinia, and Corsica and Elba, and from there soon reached all the shores of the mainland … and many lands and cities were made desolate. And the plague lasted till

- And there it stops. Villani left a blank space, clearly planning to fill in the end date of the plague. But he himself died of plague in 1348, and so the chronicle remains incomplete. Villani's brother Matteo went on to add accounts of events to the *Nuova Cronica* until he himself died in 1363—also from plague. After that, Villani's nephew Filippo briefly continued the work.

SICILY AND MARSEILLE

- The example of the island of Sicily made this clear: The plague arrived there when Genoese sailors docked in the port city of Messina in October of 1347. By the end of the year, the whole island was ravaged. Citizens of Messina fled into the Sicilian interior to escape the plague; all they did was bring it with them and spread it more quickly. The same thing happened in Pisa, which was the main port by which Tuscany accessed the Mediterranean and its trade routes.

- In this very first wave, the French port of Marseille was also struck. Marseille was the gateway to France for the plague, and from there, to England, where it struck with astonishing virulence.

- Since Marseille was an important trading hub in terms of both sea and land routes, the arrival of the Black Death there in 1347 gave the disease an advantageous position from which to advance across Western Europe.

QUESTIONS TO CONSIDER

1. Even though it was not the only—or even the primary—means of transmission of plague from east to west, why do you think the siege of Caffa has remained such a key episode in historical discussions of the Black Death?

2. How does an understanding of the trade routes of the Italian city-states in the 14th century change your understanding as to how the Black Death first affected the medieval European world?

SUGGESTED READING

Benedictow, *The Black Death 1346–1353*.

Wheelis, "Biological Warfare at the 1346 Siege of Caffa."

THE FIRST WAVE SWEEPS ACROSS EUROPE

While the siege of Caffa is memorable as one of the first and most incredible instances of biological warfare in history, it's most likely not the case that this was the only entry point by which the Black Death made its way into Western Europe. The great city of Constantinople, at the crossroads of East and West, was already suffering from a serious outbreak of plague that had most likely made it there from Hubei province in China. From these and other major trade centers, the plague moved by water across the Mediterranean and by land along caravan routes. Refugees from Caffa may indeed have brought the plague home with them, but they were not the only ones carrying the disease westward.

SICILY

- By late 1347, the port cities of Genoa, Venice, Messina, Marseille, and others were hard hit by the Black Death; in a matter of months, the sickness had radiated out from those areas as the first wave of the Black Death was cresting in Western Europe.

- Two instructive examples are the island of Sicily, off the coast of Italy, and the island of Mallorca, off the coast of the Iberian Peninsula, or what we think of today as Spain. These two areas offer a microcosmic view as to how the plague would later move throughout the rest of the continent.

- The island of Sicily is perfectly positioned as a trading center through which goods and people might move north to the Italian Peninsula; west toward France and Iberia; east toward Eastern Europe, Russia, and what we today call the Middle East; and south toward North Africa.

- Since Genoa is on the northwestern side of Italy, it made sense that Genoese sailors and merchants who were heading home from the east would stop off in Sicily to drop off goods and resupply. According to a Franciscan friar named Michele da Piazza, it was the arrival of the Genoese that brought the plague to Sicily and ravaged that island in the earliest days of the first wave.

- Michele describes the telltale buboes that erupt on the bodies of those infected, but he also says that anyone who even spoke to one of these sailors couldn't help but be infected. If that's true, then it's possible there was something else happening here other than just bubonic plague.

- Once the people of Messina realized what was happening, they expelled the sailors and their ships, but it was obviously too late. As people started falling ill, there was a run on confession and will writing, which the documentary evidence supports.

- Michele's account relates details that become all too familiar when studying the Black Death: parents refusing to care for sick children, friends abandoning their neighbors so that the dead bodies just stayed in the houses, mass graves being dug, and even thieves being afraid to enter the homes of the wealthy dead.

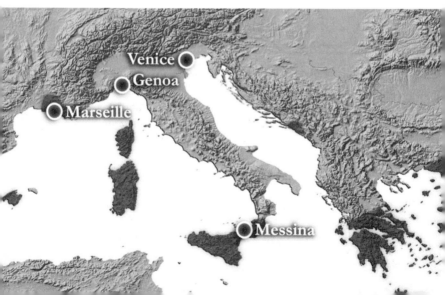

- Two groups that did, by all accounts, do their best to offer comfort were the brothers in the Franciscan and Dominican orders. These orders were notable because they "wandered" or, more simply, were deeply engaged with the world rather than sitting behind monastery walls. They used priories as home bases between their travels.

- As Michele da Piazza tells it: "The Franciscans and Dominicans, and others who were willing to visit the sick to hear their confession and impose penance, died in such large numbers that their priories were all but deserted." The Franciscans and Dominicans left the priories in order to bring comfort to the ill and dying, and then they themselves were struck down, so that there was almost no one to come back.

- Once medieval people saw what was happening, they logically figured that they should try and get away from Messina and the disease. Many of them left their homes and camped out in the vineyards around the city, and some crossed the island to the cities of Catania, Syracuse, and Calabria. But they were bringing the disease with them.

- To avoid the plague, one Duke Giovanni began wandering through the woods and wild uninhabited places, never staying more than a couple nights in one place and seeking out abandoned churches or other structures. But finally, the plague caught up to him at the Church of Sant'Andrea, where he died and was buried in April 1348.

- The duke's death marks the end of the first wave in Sicily—it had arrived in September 1347, burned its way across the island, and then finally started to peter out in April of the next year. Along the way, it took out religious leaders, government officials, and easily up to a half of the general population.

- The plague did not stay contained on Sicily; historians estimate that at the very end of 1347 or early in 1348, the plague crossed the Strait of Messina and entered the Italian Peninsula via Reggio Calabria. This would be one of the four major "bridgeheads" from which the plague would gain entrance into Italy, the other three being the port cities of Genoa, Pisa, and Venice.

MALLORCA

- From Sicily, the plague didn't just cross the Strait of Messina to the mainland—it also infected Corsica, Elba, and Sardinia. And then there's the case of Mallorca, which is very similar to that of Sicily.

- Mallorca is an island in the Mediterranean off the east coast of what we think of today as Spain. For the sake of convenience, when we talk about the medieval period, we'll call the overarching region the Iberian Peninsula.

- It had long been a very diverse region, home to Muslim communities, Christian kingdoms, and longstanding Jewish settlements, so it was carved up—like Italy—into a variety of self-governing entities that considered themselves vastly different from this community or that one just a few miles away. Mallorca, like Sicily, was an important trading hub due to its position in the Mediterranean, and it had a thriving population of around 55,000 people.

- Our best guess is that the plague made it there in December of 1347, probably coming from Marseille. Its initial progress may have been slowed by cooler weather—a pattern we see repeatedly in accounts of the Black Death. But by March 1348, the Black Death was ravaging the countryside of Mallorca.

- The plague raged on Mallorca until about May 1348, when it began to die down a bit. As was the case with Sicily and the Italian Peninsula, this also marked the moment when the disease leapt across the water barrier and made its way on to the mainland of the Iberian Peninsula. Again, it was trading ships that seem to have carried the disease with them, bringing it to the mainland via Perpignan, in what is today part of France. Then it attacked Barcelona.

BARCELONA AND VALENCIA

- Not only can we determine the extent of the plague's progress and its virulence by examining documents like chronicles, which record the incidences of infection, but we can also look at the number of religious and political offices that suddenly became vacant. Let's take the example of benefices.

- A benefice is like an appointed religious office—the Church was the biggest land-holder in the medieval world, and what it would do is grant benefices (and usually this meant control of property or land) to individuals who would carry out the work of the Church and be supported by the income from these lands and properties.

- In the religious world, whenever the holder of a benefice passed away, the Church could grant the benefice to a member of the religious community who was deserving of some kind of recognition or reward and/or was believed to be someone who would work toward the salvation of the congregation or community attached to the benefice.

- In Barcelona in April of 1348, there was one vacant benefice. In May, there were nine vacant benefices. But in June 1348, there were 25 vacancies, and then in July, there were 104 vacant benefices. Not only were those who held the benefices obviously dying of plague, but so were those who would have been logical replacements.

- Like statistics surrounding the occupation of benefices, tracking the number of wills that were being written also helps us understand the scale and virulence of the plague. In Valencia, for example, we find about two wills per year that have been preserved for the period spanning 1340–47. But in May 1348, we have surviving two wills for just that month, and then in June, that number jumps up to 21 wills—more than in the previous eight years combined.

THE PLAGUE AND THE CHURCH

- In France, after an initial infection occurring in the port city of Marseille in 1347, the plague began to move inland, with particularly devastating effects in Avignon. Avignon was at this time the seat of the papacy of the Church.

- The fact that the papal court had relocated to Avignon from Rome is why, when Italy was being devastated by plague in 1348 and 1349, Rome got by relatively unscathed. With the papacy gone, Rome had become a more rural, less cosmopolitan community. Though by modern standards it would be a charnel house, by 1348 standards, Rome was an oasis in a desert of illness and death.

- This was not the case in Avignon, as an account written by an anonymous Flemish cleric attests. He states that during the worst of the outbreak in 1348, "… in the three months from 25 January to the present day, a total of 62,000 bodies was buried in Avignon."

THE BLACK DEATH TO DATE

- While many people tend to imagine the Black Death as a line advancing from east to west across the European mainland, that's not quite right. Yes, the plague was moving along overland trade routes, but it was doing that much more slowly than it was moving along sea routes.

- In 1346, the plague showed up in the area on the northeast coast of the Black Sea, and then in early 1347 radiated north, south, and southwest— its most important point of infection at this time being the area around Constantinople, which was a center of trade, commerce, politics, religion. In other words, if the Black Death were sentient, it could not have strategized better as to where it wanted to be when it kicked things into high gear.

- As far as infection of Europe in late 1347 goes, there were key hotspots, which were all entry points or "bridgeheads" that allowed for the plague to start ravaging the mainland. In 1347, the plague, starting from the Mediterranean Sea, reached out to touch and infect Greece, the islands of Crete and Cyprus, Dubrovnik, Split, Venice, Sicily, Sardinia and the islands around it, Pisa, Genoa, Marseille, and Mallorca. It also moved to the southeast and hit Alexandria in Egypt.

- Rather than there being "waves" of plague, the situation was more like pinpricks on the geography of Europe. These made multiple little entry points by which the plague would get a foothold and start to progress inward in multiple directions. Next would come the actual waves, which would crash into each other, creating massive devastation.

QUESTIONS TO CONSIDER

1. What preconceptions about the spread of the Black Death were contradicted by the information in this lecture? What surprised you most?

2. Some chroniclers go into gruesome detail, while others make up facts, others berate their audiences for sinful behavior that must have brought on this catastrophe, and still others seem intent on only recording data, like numbers of fatalities. Why do you think there was such a variety of responses to the same phenomenon?

SUGGESTED READING

Benedictow, *The Black Death 1346–1353.*

Horrox, *The Black Death.*

The Black Death in Florence

B y this point in the course, we have a general sense of the devastation the plague wrought in its first wave on the mainland of Europe. But in this lecture, instead of broad and general descriptions, we're going to focus on one particular city to try to better understand the social, psychological, political, and economic impacts the Black Death could wreak on various communities. We're going to focus on Florence, Italy, and how that society was devastated by the plague and the interesting and varied responses that its citizens had to this onslaught.

Why Florence?

- Florence is a logical place to choose as our first case study for a variety of reasons. Of all the city-states in Italy, Florence was arguably the crown jewel. While it might seem logical that Rome would be the place of greatest development and sophistication, with the relocation of the papacy to Avignon in France in the early 1300s, Rome had lost some of its luster and power.

- By the 14th century, Florence minted its own coins. It was very wealthy, and it had its own independent governing structure. Its two major industries were banking and the wool trade, but there were many others, and for each of these there was a very powerful guild system in place.

- Florence and the lands surrounding the city proper that belonged to it—the *contado*—were the most densely populated areas of Europe at the time that the plague broke out. Most estimates give the population of the city at around 100,000 people, with the *contado* comprising an additional 300,000 people.

- Florence was an advanced community. Literary giants like Boccaccio, Dante, and Petrarch; political and economic movers like the Medici family;

and artists like Giotto, Brunelleschi, Ghiberti, and Donatello were all emerging out of 14th-century Florence.

- Florence was a deeply religious Christian community, an important consideration when we remember that when the plague struck, most religious people believed that this was God's punishment for sinful behavior.

THE PLAGUE REACHES FLORENCE

- The route the plague took to reach Florence seems most likely to have been through Pisa, with which Florence had a robust trading relationship. It probably showed up in Pisa in late 1347, and then made its way to Florence in early 1348. City records show that by April, there were 60–80 deaths due to plague occurring each day.

- The city leaders took several countermeasures:
  - On April 3, 1348, the city leaders ordered that the clothes of all sick people and those who had died be destroyed rather than sold or passed on to family members.
  - The city fathers also ordered all prostitutes out of the city. This may have been more because of concern about moral failings, and maybe a sign that some at the top were worried that sinful behavior had made God angry. (At the same time, it's pretty clear that there was an understanding that prostitution could quite easily contribute to the spread of disease.)
  - The city leaders forbade anyone from Pisa or Genoa to enter Florence. If anyone was found in violation of this rule, a huge fine would be levied.

- This was not enough to slow down the plague. The number of deaths continued to rise, so on April 11 an emergency eight-person committee was established—a medieval board of health. They were charged with making sure these rules were enforced and also that burials were carried out properly and promptly.

- But in mid-June, the death toll rose to 100 people per day, and by July and August, our best estimates are that there were 400 deaths per day from the plague. For all of 1348, it appears that the death rate was at least 20 times what would be considered normal.

- By 1352, the population of Florence proper had dropped to less than half what it had been at the start of 1348. Something like 60,000 people living in the city had died.

FLEEING TO THE COUNTRYSIDE

- Those who did not die fled to the countryside in large numbers, which led to even further depopulation of the city. One work that came out of this: The writer Giovanni Boccaccio's fictional *Decameron*, which follows 10 young nobles who have fled the city of Florence.

- In his introduction, Boccaccio relates how the horrors of the plague had turned people into terrified, panic-stricken near-animals—neighbors refusing to give assistance to those who had once been their dear friends, and parents refusing to aid their children.

- He goes at some length concerning how those at the lowest orders of society found themselves in demand. In particular, a fraternity of gravediggers unexpectedly found themselves in a position to command respect and large wages.

- Eventually, there was no choice but to resort to mass graves. A Florentine chronicler named Marchionne di Coppo Stefani described the way that bodies were laid in mass graves, with a layer of dirt, and then another layer of bodies, and then more dirt, as being similar to "how one layers lasagna with cheese."

- The problem was compounded when those who were still alive fled to the countryside, as did the fictional nobles in Boccaccio's *Decameron*. Some of these people were already infected, and brought the disease with them into the *contado*.

THE TIERS

- The city of Florence was structured rather like a pyramid, with a small group of elites at the top overseeing the merchants and guildsmen. Below them was the base of the pyramid, those who worked primarily in agriculture.

- Imagine a representative sample that has 10 people at the top, 100 in the middle, and 1,000 at the bottom. If each group loses 50 percent of its people, then the top tier is going to be less likely to adapt to or recover from its losses than the bottom, simply because of sheer numbers.

- The top was also under considerable pressure because the goods and services from the lower tiers of society suddenly increased dramatically in price. It's estimated that by the mid-1350s, the wages of skilled laborers had risen 200 percent. Unskilled laborers also benefited.

- Nobles who had the means to flee to the countryside often did so. This meant that at the top of the social order, losses might be more like 60–70 percent. The crisis of disease also quickly becomes a crisis of politics and social order, because so few people had to cope with a disaster that had affected so many.

AVOIDING CHAOS

- Given all that happened in the first wave of plague, you might expect the Florentine city-state to disintegrate into anarchy and chaos. But that's not what happened, although there were some moments when it looked like it might.

- Once the initial crisis was over, the city leaders attempted to reassert control. They passed a law dictating that those city leaders who chose to remain outside of Florence and not do their duties would be subject to a very large fine. Those who remained behind were rightly concerned that the pyramid ruling structure might be turned upside down, and the commoners might attempt to take power.

- They were right to be concerned, because this is what happened in 1378, after there had been two additional waves of plague, in an event that is known as the Ciompi revolt. Here, disaffected workers without guild representation, spearheaded by wool carders, began agitating for more power. The elites' initial, token efforts to appease them angered the Ciompi.

- In mid-July, the Ciompi took control in a wave of violence. In August, the ruling elites—the Signoria—managed to claw back some of their power, but from 1378—when the revolt broke out—to 1382, the Florentine government was essentially run by the Ciompi.

- In 1382, political pressures from outside the city, plus worsening relations between the factions of the wool dyers and wool merchants, meant that the Ciompi government was on the verge of collapsing. This made it possible for a group of people from some of the elite families in Florence to intervene and establish a new government, putting down the revolt.

CHARITABLE ASSISTANCE

- In the Middle Ages, it had long been the case that the highest mortality rates were among women and children, due to the perils of childbirth and infancy. But because plague did not discriminate, the heads of households who had long been exempt from these particular mortal dangers started dying rapidly.

- This meant there were more widows and orphans than ever before. Since this was in a patriarchal society, there was now a huge need for charitable giving directed at women and children who had no way of making a living, because it had always been presumed that there would be male family members to provide for them.

- The various governing bodies moved to provide for this newly needy population. By 1348, the Orsanmichele guild of guilds took steps to direct money from their very robust holdings of wealth to help needy widows and orphans. By 1350, other guilds were doing the same thing. They had more wealth to do so because often a single person would inherit

Sculptures at the Orsanmichele church

everything their family owned as their family died off, then leave all those possessions to their guild or parish.

RECOVERY

- Florentine leaders recognized that Florence needed its population to rebound. With that in mind, they adopted a formal policy of natalism. This means they were actively promoting marriage and childbirth. The main way to do this in 14th-century Florence was to make sure that all marriageable women had dowries that would make them attractive to potential husbands.

- Quite soon after the first terrible outbreak of plague, the leaders of Florence were working hard to restore the city to its former grand state. They gave incentives to craftsmen and artisans who were willing to move into the city from elsewhere, so that production and services that had been disrupted by the plague could be restored.

- Those people still alive were able to buy up farmland in the *contado* for bargain prices. They then made deals with surviving rural populations for a profitable sharecropping arrangement—called *mezzadria*—that would benefit both parties. The city leaders also announced the refounding of the Studio Fiorentino, a university, in an attempt to repopulate the ranks of the city's educated elites.

- Despite the best efforts of the civic and religious leaders of Florence, population levels just couldn't rebound. This was mostly due to the fact that in the second half of the 14th century, plague would return to Florence on 14 separate occasions—none as severe as the 1348 outbreak, but still disruptive.

- In 1427, it's estimated that the population of Florence was only 37 percent of what it had been in 1347, and a true demographic recovery didn't happen until quite late in the 15th century.

- Because of all the changes civic leaders of Florence had implemented in the face of the plague, by the end of the 15th century the city-state was in excellent shape once again. There was now a permanent five-person committee acting as a board of health; there were strict quarantine rules for travelers in and out of the city; and several new hospitals were constructed, one of which was specifically designated as an isolation hospital for those suspected of having contracted the Black Death.

QUESTIONS TO CONSIDER

1. Which of Florence's unique qualities affected it most positively during the period of the Black Death? Which was its greatest liability?

2. How did the guild system help the social and political infrastructure during the epidemic? How did it hurt it?

SUGGESTED READING

Byrne, *The Black Death.*

Najemy, *A History of Florence: 1200–1575.*

THE BLACK DEATH IN FRANCE

By the end of 1348, Italy and huge portions of what is today France, Spain, and Germany were suffering the effects of the Black Death. It had even crossed the English Channel and was starting its reign of terror in Britain. In this lecture, we're going to continue to track the Black Death's progress on the European continent from the end of 1348 to the beginning of 1350 and explore how several different communities dealt with it. The bulk of our attention will be spent on the part of Europe that we think of today as France, but as was the case with the Italy, a unified French identity didn't exist in the 14th century.

14TH-CENTURY FRANCE

- In 14th-century France, there was an array of powerful dukes whose power and wealth rivaled that of the actual French king. Many of them considered themselves and their realms barely part of France, if at all. The region of Burgundy is a prime example of this.

- The cultures of the north and the south of France were dramatically different. To shorthand it: the south was more liberal, more cosmopolitan, and more diverse; the north, which includes Paris, was marked by a more restrictive religious sensibility.

- Although English holdings on the continent had diminished by 1348, part of what we think of today as France was in fact England. Complicating the matter of the Black Death's presence on the continent is the fact that the French, starting in 1337, were already dealing with another kind of attack—what has come to be called the Hundred Years' War, when Edward III began to aggressively try and recover many of the territories on the continent that England had lost to France in the past.

- One more twist: Starting in 1309, the seat of the papacy moved from Rome to the southern French town of Avignon. Given all these factors, France serves as a microcosm of all the possible plague effects and responses.

THE PLAGUE IN MARSEILLE

- The plague made it to the French port city of Marseille quite early. At the very end of 1347, according to contemporary accounts, a ship from Genoa appeared at the harbor entrance.

- While other ports had begun turning away Genoese ships, the message had not made it to Marseille that ships from Genoa were starting to be recognized as carriers of the disease from the east, so the ship docked.

- The plague burned through the city with horrible ferocity, but there doesn't seem to have been the sort of mass exodus and flight out of the city like in Florence. And while Florence's political infrastructure was temporarily threatened by the ravages of the plague, the same thing doesn't seem to have happened in Marseille, even though that community saw a mortality rate of around 60 percent.

THE PLAGUE SPREADS

- From Marseille, the plague spread overland throughout France and then south into Spain through a series of what the plague scholar Ole Benedictow has called "metastatic leaps." The plague later turned back northwest. It hit Avignon, Arles, Bordeaux, Carcassone, and Lyon hard, but somehow, Carpentras, which was close to Avignon, managed to get through the pandemic pretty much unscathed.

- As the Black Death spread, people began to look for someone to blame. As has been the case so many times throughout history, the convenient scapegoat that many communities lighted upon were the Jews.

- While the town of Toulon, just east of Marseille, was the site of a horrible incident of Jewish persecution on Palm Sunday in 1348, and a harbinger of what was to come in other French communities, Marseille's response offers an exception. Scholar John Kelly wrote: "Marseille gained a reputation as a haven for Jews fleeing persecution elsewhere."

- The next community hardest hit after Marseille was Avignon. By March 1348, we estimate that around 15,000 residents of that city had died from the plague, and over 11,000 of them had been buried in a new cemetery that the pope had purchased and given to the city for the sole purpose of accommodating this tidal wave of death.

- When Avignon ran out of land, the pope actually went ahead and consecrated the Rhone River itself. Every day, hundreds of victims of plague were dumped in the river. Their bodies made their way out to the Mediterranean, where they joined up with the corpses from other towns.

BORDEAUX

- From Marseille and Avignon, the plague went to Bordeaux. Bordeaux at this time was still part of England. King Edward III of England had been actively campaigning to retake French lands for England starting in 1337.

- In 1346, Edward had launched an invasion into Normandy and had taken the city of Caen in the space of just a single day, catching the French totally off guard. On August 26, 1346, Edward's forces engaged the French army at the Battle of Crecy. The English won a stunning victory, in part because of the English longbow.

- This victory led directly to the ultimate English conquest of the port city of Calais, which would remain under English control until well into the 16th century, and also gave Edward and his advisors a burst of self-confidence.

- This may explain why, in 1348, when plague was hitting Bordeaux, Edward made a decision that in retrospect seems absolutely crazy: He sent his 15-year-old daughter, Princess Joan, there for a stopover on her way to the Kingdom of Castile. She was on her way there because Edward intended to marry Joan to the kingdom's heir, Prince Pedro.

King Edward III of England

- Among Joan's attendants were the high-ranking diplomat Robert Bourchier and Andrew Ullford, who was a battle-hardened veteran of many wars, including the recent fight at Crecy.

- When the English ships put in at Bordeaux in August 1348, there was death everywhere. As in the rest of the medieval world during the first wave of the epidemic, 50–60 percent of the population died of the plague.

- In fact, the mayor of the town told the English entourage that they should not land in Bordeaux because they might die. But for whatever reason, Bourchier and Ullford ignored this warning, and the royal wedding party promptly took up lodgings in the Palais de l'Ombriere, which was a stately castle with a lovely view looking right over Bordeaux's harbor. Harbors are an ideal place for infected fleas to hitch a ride from one place to another.

- The next part is predictable: By all accounts, Joan and her escorts died horrible, agonizing deaths from plague. Only Ullford survived. He had the unpleasant task of reporting to the king that his daughter had died of plague, and with her, England's chance for an alliance with Castile.

THE PLAGUE IN PARIS

- The plague made it to Paris relatively late. It was probably sometime in August 1348 that the Black Death found its way into the city, and the effects were, as everywhere, utterly devastating.

- If Florence was the most densely populated city in the medieval world at this time, Paris was the largest metropolis, with about 200,000 inhabitants. Paris was the site of one of the first universities in the medieval world, and it had, by the standards of the day, an impressive medical faculty, whom the French king called upon to figure out what was going on.

- The 46 masters of medicine at the University of Paris produced one of the most important scientific works concerning the Black Death, the

Compendium de epidemia per collegium facultatis medicorum Parisius, which is fascinating for the emphasis it places on how earthquakes, floods, unseasonable weather, planetary conjunctions, and "bad air" contributed to the outbreak of plague.

- While the tract provides fascinating insight into medieval medical theory, it was basically useless for those who were suffering through the Black Death—a fact that is underscored by the fact that pretty much all of the authorities who worked on the *Compendium* died of plague themselves.

- But the important thing about the *Compendium* is the approach it shows: Instead of fleeing the city, or blaming a population like the Jews—which couldn't happen in Paris, because all its Jews had been expelled some time before—here we see people turning to the greatest minds of their day to try and understand the plague.

- And it wasn't just the medical faculty of the university who felt compelled to offer written commentary on the plague. It's estimated that between 1348 and 1350 there were some 24 plague tracts written by a variety of people. Some of these were decidedly quirky by modern standards—one medical treatise was even written in poetic verse.

- An English medical authority named John Colle, taking the Paris medical faculty's statement about bad air as a starting point, theorized that the best way to counteract bad air that carried infection was with more bad air. This led to the bizarre sight of people gathered around public latrines, inhaling deeply, thinking that *this* bad smell would act as protection against whatever bad smell was carrying the plague with it.

- While the majority of the population of Paris did not flee the city, there was an exception—the French king Philip VI took a page out of the Florentine playbook and hightailed it out of there, moving around the countryside in a game of hide-and-seek with the Black Death. He escaped, dying of natural causes in 1350, but his queen did not.

RESPONSES

- Those who remained in Paris chronicled the horrors of the epidemic. One Jean de Venette recounted how the hospital of the Hôtel-Dieu was particularly hard hit. Its population was made up of those who were already ill or elderly, and the quarters were pretty close—multiple patients sometimes shared a single bed.

- These were prime conditions for the Black Death. Says de Venette: "The mortality was so great that, for a considerable period, more than 500 bodies a day were being taken in carts from the Hôtel-Dieu in Paris for burial in the cemetery of the Holy Innocents."

- Other sources similarly confirm the high mortality rates. In the words of historian John Kelly: "During the eighteen months between June 1348 and December 1349, Paris seems to have lost the equivalent of a good-sized village almost every day, and on bad days, a good-sized town."

- This state of affairs eventually led to a new kind of response to the plague: indifference. About a year or so into the first wave of the Black Death, resignation set in in Paris, Marseille, Avignon, and scores of other communities.

- But in a few places, there was a response that seems awfully like tempting fate. One of these episodes is recounted in the *Grandes Chroniques de France,* or *Great Chronicle of France*, which was kept by the monks of Saint-Denis, just outside Paris. In this particular account, the chronicler tells that two monks from the abbey were traveling through the countryside at the behest of their abbot, when they encountered a village in which all the people were dancing to the music of drums and bagpipe.

- The villagers explained that "… since the plague has not entered our town, we hope that our merrymaking will keep it away, and this is why we are dancing." But on their way back home, the monks passed through the same village, and everyone seemed very sad.

- This time, the explanation was: "Alas, good lords, the wrath of God came upon us in a hailstorm, for a great hailstorm came from the sky and fell on our town and all around, so suddenly that some people were killed by it, and others died of fright, not knowing where to go or which way to turn."

- The merry-making response to plague would show up throughout the medieval world as the plague made its way across the continent. On other occasions, people turned the opposite way and, in acts of religious devotion, sought to further punish and humiliate their flesh in the hope that this would appease the wrath of God.

QUESTIONS TO CONSIDER

1. How do the variety of cultural identities at play in 14th-century France seem to have affected responses to the plague?

2. Which responses seem to be the most unexpected from a modern perspective? Which responses do you think make the most sense from a medieval perspective?

SUGGESTED READING

Aberth, *The Black Death*.

Horrox, *The Black Death*.

THE BLACK DEATH IN AVIGNON

I n this lecture, we're going to do a case study of the city of Avignon. Located in the south of France, it was hit by the plague shortly after the Black Death came to Marseille. In many respects, the experience of Avignon is very similar to what happened in other cities that were struck early on. But at the same time, Avignon is an exceptional case because at this point it was not just another city in France or in continental Europe. It was the seat of the papacy, which meant that all kinds of questions about mortality, religion, governance, medicine, and literature—not to mention some big personalities— intersected when the epidemic hit Avignon.

BACKGROUND ON AVIGNON

- In the early 14th century, the French king Philip IV got embroiled in a nasty feud with Pope Boniface VIII. The feud centered around a by-now familiar conflict over Church powers versus state powers: Who had control over the clergy, the king or the pope in Rome? Philip thought it was he who should be the overlord of members of the clergy in France; Boniface thought that the papacy and its concerns overrode those of any secular ruler.

- Philip is the king who famously rounded up the Knights Templar, tortured them to confess to hideous acts they certainly never committed, confiscated their considerable wealth, and executed them. Boniface was interested mostly in power and money, and to that end made a brisk business selling Church appointments and indulgences, acts for which Dante Alighieri famously put him in the 8th circle of hell in his *Divine Comedy*.

- In 1305, following the death of Boniface's successor, who was pope for only a few months, the papal enclave met and eventually elected as pope Clement V. He was French, and decided that he was not going to go to Rome—instead, he would stay in France.

- All the infrastructure of the papacy, including the clergy, lawyers, politicians, advisors, and other staff, suddenly had to be moved and overlaid and worked into the infrastructure of Clement's home base of Avignon. The population of Avignon more than doubled, and those who made up the new members of this community were mostly foreigners, many of whom eventually married into the local population.

- For seven popes, over the years of 1309–1377, the seat of the Church in Western Europe was in Avignon. Thus it was when plague struck in 1348, during the reign of Pope Clement VI.

- None of the Avignon popes were fans of the monastic virtues like poverty and chastity. Scholar John Kelly notes that, in addition to an obscenely lavish and hedonistic lifestyle, the papacy in Avignon under the first 14th-century French pope, Clement V, had "transformed the Church into a spiritual Pez dispenser." Anything you wanted, any sin you wanted to commit or rule you wanted to break, could be had for a price. Clement VI was particularly notorious in this regard.

- Because of the mistral wind, which deposited dust everywhere, if you were doing bureaucratic work, you had to be inside with the shutters closed. Even during the middle of the day you had to work by candlelight. At the end of the day, Church officials alleviated this stressful situation by going drinking, or to a brothel, or both. It's instructive to note that Avignon had 11 whorehouses at this time, while Rome only had two.

THE PLAGUE ARRIVES

- The plague made its entrance onto the Avignon stage in January 1348. When it first showed up, it appeared to be the pneumonic form. Later, as the epidemic continued, we have documentation that indicates the bubonic form was also showing up. This suggests that people carrying the pneumonic form brought the plague to Avignon from Marseille first, and that the rats and their infected fleas made their way to the papal seat a little bit later.

- A personal letter from a Flemish man named Louis Heyligen contained an account of the horrors of the plague; the letter made it north to friends and family ahead of the Black Death. It contained a description of the fateful Genoese galley that docked at Marseilles, as well as an account of the pope purchasing a large plot of land for a cemetery.

- By March of 1348—not even three whole months since the Black Death's arrival—over 11,000 people had been buried there. The unceasing onslaught of death is what led Clement to finally consecrate the Rhone River so that the bodies of plague victims could be buried there, as there was no more room left on land.

- The river seems to have been a sensible solution that took care of another problem as well. Many accounts report after a mass burial took place, in the evening wild pigs and dogs would get into the cemetery and root around the bodies, dragging some of them—or parts of them—back out into the open.

- Heyligen's letter also gives us some fascinating details about steps people took to protect themselves from the plague. For example, he notes "no kinds of spices are eaten or handled, unless they have been in stock for a year, because men are afraid that they might have come from the galleys of which I spoke." There was also scapegoating, with some men being burned for supposedly poisoning wells with powders.

RELIGIOUS REACTIONS

- In March, when the epidemic was reaching full steam, the pope granted a plenary indulgence, which was good until Easter, for all who died of plague. He even took the extraordinary step of decreeing that if someone found him or herself on the point of death, last confession could be made to anyone who was present, whether or not they were clergy—even if the person hearing confession was a woman.

- There were also extra church services and religious processionals throughout the town, many of which the pope himself took part in. These processions were some of the first instances when we see the rise in the popularity of the flagellant movement.

- Dressed in little more than rags, the flagellants beat themselves with whips and scourges until the blood ran in copious amounts, the idea being that they would punish their own flesh in an attempt to atone for the fleshly sins of all mankind.

- Although he had tolerated the flagellants at first, in 1349 Clement VI issued a papal bull condemning the practice, which he sent out to all the bishops in Western Europe. Despite this, the movement continued to exist and, in some places, flourish, especially during the years of the Black Death.

THE POPE'S STRATEGY

- While the pope, as the head of the Church, was certainly expected to offer prayers for God's mercy and comfort to those in his religious flock, he himself doesn't necessarily seem to have viewed the epidemic as a punishment from God—or at the very least, he was hedging his bets.

- Even as Clement attended to the spiritual needs and emotional comfort of his flock, he also was interested in the scientific and medical causes of the epidemic. He had a huge medical and scientific staff on hand, and he consulted them regarding the Black Death. He was very interested when his astrologers explained the outbreak in part as being due to a planetary conjunction.

- He also issued a papal bull condemning the persecution of the Jews, noting that while, yes, it was lamentable that they were nonbelievers, they were one of God's chosen people, and Jesus had been born to a Jewish mother. He also pointed out that the Jews in Avignon were dying in numbers equivalent to non-Jews, which made it doubtful that they were behind the outbreak.

- He followed the main recommendation of his doctors, which was to confine himself to his chambers and have two huge bonfires lit at either end of the room. This may have been why he did not contract the plague:

He was quarantined from human pneumonic plague carriers, and the bonfires kept rats and fleas away.

- But finally, as Heyligen tells us in his letter, the pope decided to leave Avignon for the city of Etoile-sur-Rhone, where the plague had not yet arrived. Heyligen indicates that his immediate master, one Cardinal Giovanni Colonna, was planning to go along, which meant Heyligen would be going, too.

- What happened to Heyligen, we don't know for sure, but we do know that Cardinal Colonna never made it out of the city, succumbing to plague in July 1348. He was in good company—it's estimated that 50–55 percent of Avignon's population (so around 60,000 people) died before the plague finally began to abate. A quarter to a third of Clement's papal officials succumbed to plague.

- Somewhat surprisingly, Clement ultimately opted not to leave Avignon, and he eventually came out from between his fires to minister last rites, oversee burials, and tend to the physical and spiritual needs of his flock.

- When Clement VI finally died of a non-plague-related hemorrhage in 1352—still in Avignon—his body was laid in state. He was memorialized as a man of fine taste and culture, a patron of the arts and education, and a gentleman with excellent manners—but definitely not a saint.

- Another person who stayed in the city was the pope's personal physician, Guy de Chauliac. It is from de Chauliac that we get detailed descriptions of the symptoms of the Black Death, including the nature of buboes, which he calls *apostemes*. At the end of his account of the plague in Avignon, he adds that he survived his own infection.

- De Chauliac lived on into 1368. His case is fascinating in that it is absolutely clear that he had contracted the bubonic form of the plague, and it confirms what other sources and scientific research have indicated: This form of plague was survivable, although the odds were not particularly good.

QUEEN JOANNA

- In March 1348, when the plague was approaching its peak, Queen Joanna of Naples and Sicily, who was also countess of Provence, chose to enter Avignon not only despite the plague but in some sense because of it.

- Joanna was accused of arranging and perhaps participating in the murder of her husband, Prince Andrew of Hungary, in 1345. Although Joanna was reportedly distraught and wept when told the news, Prince Andrew's family was suspicious, and they held her responsible for her husband's death.

- Thus, Joanna opted to travel to Avignon for a hearing in the papal court to clear her name. The fact that plague was well known to be ravaging the city actually acted in her favor, as she and her supporters continually pointed out that her willingness to go there was further testament to her innocence.

- Despite some seemingly incriminating evidence at the trial, Joanna was declared "above suspicion of guilt." The pope embraced her before the entire gathering; the Hungarians gritted their teeth and bore it, but they did not forget.

- In 1382, 37 years after Andrew's death, a Hungarian agent snuck up behind Joanna while she was kneeling in prayer and strangled her to death. The Hungarians were angry because just a few months after the trial, Clement cut a very favorable deal to take possession of the city of Avignon itself, purchasing it from the title holder—Joanna—for the bargain price of 80,000 gold florins.

- After this, the papacy and Avignon were even more tightly connected. But this connection was not to last. In 1378 Pope Gregory XI moved the pontificate back to Rome. He died shortly thereafter, and this led to the event known as the Great Schism, during which time there might be two or three rival popes in existence at the same time. Two of these "antipopes" held their positions in Avignon in a last-gasp effort to cling to what had been established there, but they eventually lost out.

QUESTIONS TO CONSIDER

1. How does the presence of the papacy in Avignon seem to alter the plague experience there?

2. What surprised you most about the responses of the population to the Black Death in this capital of Christendom?

SUGGESTED READING

Kelly, *The Great Mortality.*

Rollo-Koster, *Avignon and Its Papacy, 1309–1417.*

THE BLACK DEATH IN ENGLAND

The year 1348 was not a very good one in Europe. The Black Death was ravaging the medieval world. This lecture is about the epidemic's impact on England. It starts with background on England at the time, focusing on circumstances that made the area particularly vulnerable to plague. The lecture then moves on to the plague's arrival in England. Finally, the lecture looks at mortality rates, how the plague affected different classes of people, and the Black Death's ongoing impact on England.

ENGLAND'S SITUATION

- Contemporary accounts from England describe several instances of the telltale buboes appearing in the groin and armpits of infected individuals, but there are also rather shocking tallies of dead animals, and specific references to a murrain that wiped out huge herds of livestock. The plague affected both human and animal populations in Florence, but in England the accounts are rather extreme; some wonder if this points to anthrax, an unidentified zoonotic disease, or a viral, hemorrhagic fever.

- Prior to the arrival of the Black Death in England, there was a perfect storm of circumstances that made that region both an ideal incubator for disease in the physical sense and in a social and economic sense.

- Extreme amounts of rain made for a poor harvest. This worsened nutritional instability that was already present thanks to England's doubling in population over the previous two centuries.

- This situation might also explain why there was such a huge die-off of sheep and cattle—the unusual weather had maybe created a situation in which certain infectious diseases were made into superbugs. Or, as some have theorized, it may have somehow exposed people and livestock to new viruses with which they had not come in contact before.

- We also know that there had been an earthquake reported near York in late 1348, which may have displaced some rodent populations who were carriers of plague and other diseases.

- In the first half of the 14th century, a land crunch had made the agrarian life of subsistence farming no longer a possibility for many people. By the middle of the 14th-century in England, the society as a whole had started to move into an economy that was more specialized and cash-based.

- People became tanners, blacksmiths, butchers, cobblers, and so on. We have the start of the rise of merchant class who make their living almost exclusively as part of a cash economy.

- They might import and export wine, or wool, or spices—and with their income, they purchase the foodstuffs they need to survive, rather than growing their own food. All of this would have been just fine, and the economy might have kept on chugging along in this fashion, except for the arrival of the Black Death. This was a black swan event—something completely outside the realm of normal expectations.

The Plague Arrives

- In England, the death toll in most places was equivalent to that found on the continent—right around 50 percent, but in some communities mortality might have been as high 70–80 percent. With mortality rates that high, all the practitioners of a certain specialized craft or trade could get wiped out along with their apprentices.

- As throughout Europe, the plague first arrived in England through a port city. The chronicle known as the "Greyfriars' Chronicle" notes that the plague arrived in Weymouth sometime in June 1348 on a ship that had come from Gascony—the part of France that included Bordeaux, which was the place where the princess Joan had died of plague on her journey to be married to Prince Pedro of Castile.

- From Weymouth, the plague was carried by ship south and west around Cornwall, breaking out in full force in Bristol in August 1348. Next was Gloucester. Although the leaders of this city recognized what was happening and tried to quarantine the city by shutting the gates against any travelers, it was too late.

- From this point on, the Black Death spread rapidly throughout England. England's water-based trade networks allowed the plague to advance quickly along the coasts and inland. Because fishing was a huge industry in England, it's pretty clear that fishing vessels were spreading the Black Death all along the coastal waterways as well.

- London was spared until relatively late—plague didn't show up there in full force until the beginning of 1349. Once it arrived, however, it made up for lost time with its incredible virulence.

- From the bridgeheads of Gloucester and Weymouth, the plague made what plague expert Ole Benedictow has called a "three-pronged attack" on the city of London.

- › From Gloucester, the plague was heading overland southeastward along the road from that city to London.
- › From Weymouth, it was heading along the main road that ran northeast, passing through Salisbury and Winchester.
- › The third prong came in through the harbor.

- In later 1348 we have the first indication that some deaths in London were occurring due to plague; by 1349, the three prongs of Black Death had fully converged on London, crashing into each other, overlapping, and leaving a grim trail of death and destruction.

TRACKING THE PLAGUE

- One way we can track the plague's progression is through records about the need to fill vacant clerical offices. In the towns along the south and west coast, we see a surge in clerical vacancies in the autumn of 1348. The priests were hard hit because they were visiting parishioners who were ill and in need of comfort and last rites. Other scholars point out that those in clerical benefices were likely to be older and more susceptible to illness to begin with.

- Additionally, the plague burned through monasteries. Many people living together in close quarters is a perfect recipe for an epidemic. The abbey of Meaux lost 83 percent of its population, with 42 out of 52 monks and all of the lay brothers attached to the monastery perishing.

- Wills are another way to track the epidemic. We see a sharp increase in wills written and filed in January 1349, which suggests that the noble classes had started to feel threatened by the epidemic in the late autumn of 1348.

LOSSES

- Once the plague had gained a foothold in London, there was no escaping the Black Death in Britain. By 1349 it had swept through all of England and moved into Wales. The Scots on the border, at first spared by the outbreak, decided in 1350 that now was the time to invade the lands to the south.

These plans changed dramatically when the plague found its way into the ranks of the invading army and killed 5,000 of them almost overnight.

- The losses in England were staggering. Of a population of 60,000 in London at the start of the epidemic, less than half that number were still in the city by 1351—probably due to a combination of deaths and flight from the urban setting.

- Nobles were somewhat less affected than the peasants, probably due to the fact that many of their houses were built of stone, which was less easily penetrated by flea-carrying rats than the wood structures in which the peasant classes lived. They also had better nutrition and were healthier to start with.

- The losses among the noble classes were probably somewhere around 25–30 percent, and among the peasants could run anywhere from 40–70 percent, with some places recording mortality rates as high as 80 percent. The priestly classes had losses of around 45 percent.

SOCIAL IMPACTS

- The Black Death produced some situations that had to be coped with in new ways. For example, whenever the head of a peasant family living on an English lord's manor died, his family owed the lord a heriot, or death tax. This usually took the form of the family's best animal.

- Because of the Black Death, suddenly the lords had more animals than they could cope with. With this sudden influx of livestock available for the taking, the value and prices for such animals plummeted. Lords with more animals than they knew what to do with dumped them on to the open market, which further depressed prices.

- Whole families had been wiped out, and there weren't enough bodies to work the land—a situation that resulted in skyrocketing prices for labor.

- Although London quickly ran out of burial space and had to consecrate new plots of land as mass graves, it was not the case that people were simply dumping bodies into a hole in the ground. Recent archaeological excavations of so-called plague pits show that even though they were mass graves, the bodies were usually laid out in orderly fashion—all oriented in the same direction, sometimes grouped together by age and gender.

RELIGION

- Religious institutions did not fare so well during the epidemic. Not only did the monasteries suffer huge losses, but England had two archbishops die of plague, one of whom succumbed just 40 days after his consecration, which had been hastily arranged because his predecessor had just died of the Black Death.

- Clergy refused to visit those who were ill and suffering, so great was their terror of being sickened themselves. When they did perform their duties, like administering last rites, many of them did so both hastily and reluctantly—a fact that would not have endeared them to the families of the people who were ill.

- There were many devoted priests who bravely performed their duties sincerely and generously to the fullest of their abilities—but because they did this, and were exposed to plague on numerous occasions, those good men of the cloth were some of the first to die.

- People were desperate to find some explanation for God's wrath. Apart from the pseudoscientific claims about the conjunction of planets and bad air spreading the infection, God's wrath was the obvious cause. In Henry Knighton's account, he blames the recent vogue in tournaments and the scandalous clothing worn by those in attendance.

SLOWDOWN

- Although the first wave of the plague finally slowed down by the end of 1350, there was no way for the populace to know this. In 1348, when the plague arrived, it may have seemed like a one-time epidemic; because the black rat fleas go into hibernation in winter, the rate of infection of the bubonic type seemed to slow down.

- But then it came roaring back with a vengeance in the summer of 1349, and again in the summer of 1350. There was no reason for people to doubt that this was now going to be the new normal, so it must have seemed like an answer to a prayer when 1351 was almost plague-free.

- However, the plague kept coming back once every 6–10 years or so. There were over 15 recurrences of the Black Death in England between 1351 and 1485. The plague outbreak of 1361 was an incredibly traumatic recurrence, as the majority of the victims were the children of survivors of the first pandemic.

- In the long term, there was a combination of high mortality and low birth rate, since many women delayed marriage and childbearing after the first outbreak because they were needed in the labor force. England's population would not recover to pre-plague levels until well into the 16th century.

QUESTIONS TO CONSIDER

1. How does England's experience of the Black Death seem different from the continental experience of plague?

2. Of the economic, social, and religious spheres, which one seems to have suffered the most? Which one changed the most? Which group in English society benefitted the most from the plague?

SUGGESTED READING

Gottfried, *The Black Death.*

Platt, *King Death.*

THE BLACK DEATH IN WALSHAM

I n this lecture, we're going to examine the rural English village of Walsham in Suffolk. We'll be focusing on Walsham in this case study for a couple of reasons. One is that Walsham is quite a typical English community. It was, technically speaking, a manor—a type of social organization particularly entrenched in England. Under this system, the manor and the lands around it—the *fief*—were owned by a lord, and on that land lived peasants who were bound to the lord by oaths of service and the promise of protection. Another reason we're focusing on Walsham is that it's one of the few communities that has reliable records that precede the onslaught of plague and continue during the worst of the outbreak.

THE BLACK DEATH: AN INTIMATE HISTORY

- The medieval and early modern scholar John Hatcher of Cambridge University wrote one of the most famous and innovative treatments of Walsham. Hatcher's treatment of Walsham is so innovative because it takes an approach somewhere between historical analysis and historical fiction. In *The Black Death: An Intimate History*, Hatcher relies as much as possible on concrete facts, events, and numbers to paint a picture of what happened at Walsham in 1348.

- Hatcher also invents dialogue and reconstructs events that must have taken place even when he's not entirely sure of the details. For instance, Hatcher invents a name for a priest whose actual name has been lost to posterity.

- Hatcher's experiment in writing about the Black Death this way—not to mention the widespread attention his work has received and the wealth of information he brings to light—means that it is impossible to talk about the Black Death and not talk about Hatcher's analysis of what happened in Walsham.

WALSHAM

- Walsham was a little unusual as far as the manorial system goes in that there were essentially two noble households in control of the lands, making this area two manors run side by side.
  - The bigger of the properties was Walsham Manor. For the period in question, this belonged to Lady Rose de Valognes, who had inherited it from her father. Lady Rose married twice, and held the property on her own after the death of her second husband, who succumbed to plague. She was not in residence there, however, so the running of her estate would have been the domain of a reeve, or professional estate manager.
  - The other estate, whose seat was High Hall, was smaller and occupied by Sir Nicholas Walsham. When he died in 1347, his widow, Margery, and her brother Edmund de Welles took over.

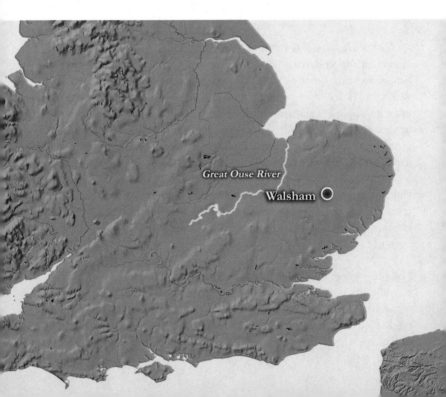

- When the Black Death came to Walsham, that community looked a lot like the rest of the medieval world at this point. It was enduring a land crunch, as the population had risen and available land was scarce.

- There were a few families who held large numbers of acres and were thus relatively well off. Most members of the community—and there were over 1,000 in 1340—held just enough land to scratch out a bit more than subsistence living. At the bottom of the hierarchy were peasants who had to pay relatively high rents for very small garden plots and who were forced to hire themselves out for manual labor.

- The community was primarily agricultural, but Walsham was also part of a commercial network that included the nearby abbey of Bury St. Edmunds abbey. Bury St. Edmunds also had one of the wealthiest monasteries in England.

- On the eve of the arrival of the Black Death, Bury St. Edmunds had a thriving scholastic community that housed some 70–80 monks. It had one of the finest libraries in the land, and scholars and Church officials regularly traveled there to make study and consult the manuscripts held in its library.

- These regular visits by people who traveled throughout England and came from abroad meant that there was a stable communication network in place, which in turn meant this place would have received the horrifying news about the Black Death long before the plague actually arrived.

THE ARRIVAL

- At the Walsham Manor court of March 6, it was recorded that there had been no deaths since the last court hearing of about two months before. At the next session, which was held on June 15th, there were 103 recorded deaths.

- This doesn't sound too bad. After all, if the population was around 1,100 people, then this would seem to be a mortality rate of around 10 percent—low by Black Death standards.

- But those numbers only record heads of households. If the evidence of plague we've seen so far is any indicator, then when one family member succumbed to the Black Death, so did most others. One scholar estimates that a way to get a conservative estimate would be to take the figure of 103 and multiply it by four to get an actual body count; other scholars suggest multiplying by a factor of six or even seven.

RUNNING WALSHAM

- The orderly running of the manor became extremely complicated. In normal times, after the death of a tenant, that tenant's heir would have the right to step forward and claim the tenancy, or negotiate with the lord— maybe giving it up for a sum, or perhaps claiming it and then renting it out to someone else who could work it.

- If it so happened that no heir was to be found, the situation could usually be managed—a vacant tenancy here and there was actually somewhat desirable, as that land could be reassigned or rented out, and this would help ease the land crunch. But in the aftermath of the plague, in June of 1349, the supply and demand graph at Walsham was turned upside down.

- In his book, Hatcher paints a vivid picture of what must have happened at the manor court meeting of June 15. The surviving tenants would have most likely gathered in Lady Rose's barn. The crowd gathered Walsham would have noticed that most of people they were used to seeing run these meetings—the reeve, the clerk of the court, and so on—were absent because they were dead.

- We can imagine they were relieved to see at least one familiar face in the room—the steward, John Blakey. Their relief most likely turned to horror, however, when his first announcement was that Sir Hugh de Saxham, Lady Rose's husband, had died of plague. What happened next would be very similar to what was happening all over the medieval world: the attempt to get on with business as usual.

- The next step would be to read out the roll of those who had died. The family of that person would be expected to identify what they planned to offer as the heriot, or death tax, to the estate. After that, there would be the matter of deciding who could claim a vacant tenancy, and what terms of transfer would be required to complete the transaction.

- According to the records of that day, the first of these death announcements and transfers went smoothly. The next, however, did not. Adam Hardonn, who had held the tenancy of a cottage with a garden, had his name read. No one stepped forward. Someone stated for the record that Adam had a brother, William, who should be the heir, and furthermore, William knew both about his brother's death and had been aware that the court was scheduled to convene that day, but William had not shown up.

- The court decreed that William was to be tracked down and compelled to take over his brother's holding and pay all the taxes that were due. And after that piece of official business, the process really did not go smoothly at all.

- As each name of the dead was read aloud, the assembled group would probably have turned collectively to look for the heir to the dead man to step forward. But even as they turned to look, they might have all realized, "Oh, wait, he's dead, too."

- In the Deneys family, the patriarch, Walter, had been one of the first to die. His property had passed to his son, Robert, but then he died, too. It had then passed to his son John, who stepped forward on June 15th to pledge loyalty to Lady Rose and claim lands that had, until recently, been two generations removed from his possession.

- Another member of the extended Deneys family, Nicholas, is an example of how the plague could confer great good fortune in the midst of horrible bad luck. He inherited so much from various dead relatives that he eventually turned down a holding from a distant relative.

- In other instances, the heirs of a deceased tenant were found to be young children who had been orphaned by the plague. The court proceedings of June 15th spent a great deal of time identifying several orphans who were also heirs, and then trying to find suitable guardians for all of them.

- While the guardianship issues seemed to have been satisfactorily resolved that day, the labor issue most definitely was not—how could a nine-year-old or a three-year-old be considered a head of household responsible for the heavy labor of farming?

ATTEMPTS AT NORMALCY

- In the weeks that followed the June 15th assembly, those still living at Walsham attempted to get things back to normal as quickly as possible. This proved easier said than done, as the shortage of laborers everywhere not only made working the land difficult but made filling key positions on the manor hard as well.

- The key to a successful and profitable manor was an honest and competent reeve, or overseer. Walsham's reeve—along with several other officials—had died. According to court records, in the High Hall proceedings in 1350, one John Packard was elected reeve of the estate. He refused to accept the position, for reasons that have been lost to us, but it may have had something to do with the fact that, in the aftermath of the plague, getting a manor like Walsham up and running at full strength again was likely to be an overwhelming endeavor.

- In the wake of the plague it was a laborer's market—there was lots of land and not enough people to work it, which meant that for the first time in centuries, a peasant could decide to head down the road to another estate and ask for higher wages if he or she didn't like the compensation offered at a particular manor.

- The English government tried to step in and stop this from happening by passing a law known as the Statute of Laborers in 1351. This statute froze wages at pre-plague levels and forbade people from moving around the countryside without license, among other things.

- The records show that in 1353 there was a huge pushback from the peasant population at Walsham—many peasants refused to labor, and some relocated entirely. But these acts of defiance against the lords of Walsham didn't happen until relatively late—remember, the Statute of Laborers was in place by 1351, and similar laws had been decreed as early as 1350.

- 1353 was also the year that Lady Rose died. This suggests that the Walsham tenants' bonds to the manor were not just about land, but also about a personal relationship. It seems likely that when that personal relationship was over, the desire to adhere to earlier loyalties evaporated.

QUESTIONS TO CONSIDER

1. How does examining the experience of plague at Walsham help us better understand both the plague and the society it affected?

2. Is Hatcher's approach—straddling history and fiction—a useful one for a subject such as this?

SUGGESTED READING

Hatcher, *The Black Death.*

Kelly, *The Great Mortality.*

THE BLACK DEATH IN SCANDINAVIA

After Italy was overrun in 1348, the Great Pestilence moved northward overland, striking the German-speaking countries, and then crept farther north still into parts of Scandinavia. That wave would crash into another current of plague that entered Denmark via trade networks with Norway. In this lecture, we're going to focus on Scandinavia and its experience of the Great Mortality. First, we'll get some background on how the plague reached Scandinavia, and how Scandinavian society had particular vulnerabilities to it. Then we'll look at unique responses to the Black Death that appeared in Scandinavia.

SCANDINAVIA AND THE PLAGUE

- Different parts of Scandinavia were infected at different times and by different routes, so by one measure it might not make sense to talk about the "Scandinavian experience" of plague.

- By another measure, it makes total sense because the "Scandinavian experience" was marked by a fascinating folktale response in which the Black Death was anthropomorphized variously into an old woman, a pair of children, an old man, and in some cases frightening animals, like a three-legged goat with blazing eyes. These depictions seem to be found nowhere else—they are culturally unique to Norway, Sweden, Denmark, and Finland.

- The fifth Scandinavian country, Iceland, had a different experience with plague. It escaped the first wave of the Black Death and didn't experience plague until 1402.

THE INFECTION'S SOURCE

- Various forms of bubonic plague are what caused most of the high death rate in Scandinavia between 1349 and 1351. The source of the infection has been identified by many sources as a specific ship carrying wool to Norway that departed London in May 1349, probably intending to arrive and unload its cargo in Oslo. Somewhere en route, plague swept through the ship—one of the crew must have been infected but didn't know it before embarking.

- Numerous accounts say that the whole crew died and the ship sailed on and drifted until it ran aground somewhere near Bergen. Other accounts say the ship didn't run aground at all but was spotted drifting by people on shore somewhere on the west coast of Norway. Curious, they rowed out to see what had happened, and then brought the disease back with them. Still other accounts suggest that the some of the crew had died but the remainder made it to Norway, where, while they were still alive, they infected the local residents.

- The image of the rudderless ghost ship with all hands lost to plague is certainly one of the most compelling images to come out of the story of the infection of Scandinavia, but some doubt that a drifting ship could have made it all the way to Bergen without running aground earlier. Still, it's not impossible that the infection happened this way.

- No matter the details, what is certain is that the plague came to Norway from England via ship in late spring 1349. And from this account, it seems clear that plague was striking the islands off of what we think of today as Scotland before becoming a presence in the interior of that realm.

THE SPREAD

- When it comes to the spread of plague through Scandinavia, the trade routes are the culprits. In general, the Scandinavian sociopolitical system was somewhat different from the rest of Western Europe in that feudalism was not as strongly or deeply pervasive.

- While still a primarily agricultural society, the land was mostly freely held—rather than in fee or vassalage from the king or a lord—and there were many who lived in mountain settlements where agriculture could not offer a subsistence existence.

- Those who lived in the mountains were dependent on extensive trade networks running down to the coast for many of the goods they required for survival, and it's along these routes that the plague made its way inland through Norway and thence to Sweden and finally to Denmark, which was also suffering from plague coming up from the south.

- Scandinavia's agricultural system was particularly dependent upon young, unwed men—known as *ungkarl*, or *ungkarlar* plural—as labor. This was different from a place like England, where a family unit performed agriculture, with the oldest male—the father or head of the household—being arguably the most important component of the feudal, manorial structure.

- In Scandinavia, while it was necessary for young men to marry and reproduce in order to carry on the production of society, marrying too young was not ideal, because that took a man out of the *ungkarl* labor pool. When the Black Death swept through Scandinavia, it carried off many young men and women who were, of course, the producers of the next generation.

- The Scandinavian agricultural system was further damaged when, in response to the onslaught of the Black Death, there was another demographic shift—people started marrying younger, which once again diminished the *ungkarl* labor pool.

- Interestingly, this seems to be the opposite of what happened in response to plague in England and other parts of Western Europe. There, the average age at which people chose to marry went up.

- Perhaps the most terrifying thing about the plague was that even those in as yet unaffected regions knew it was coming. For example, in 1350 King Magnus of Sweden issued a letter to his people warning them of the Great Mortality that was moving their way, saying God had brought it for the "sins of men." The king goes on to call for fasting on Fridays, processionals through the cities, and other acts of penance and atonement, all in the hope of appeasing God.

- Magnus's measures didn't work. From Italy to Ireland and from France to Denmark, the Black Death's conquest of Europe was complete once Sweden succumbed in 1350. In 1351–1353, the plague would complete its deathly journey by heading east and south through Poland into Russia, and ending up almost exactly where it had begun.

RESPONSES TO THE PLAGUE

- Though in many accounts from Italy and France and elsewhere the speaker or writer talks of family members abandoning ill loved ones or neighbors out of fear of the plague, in Scandinavia this did not happen at first. In the first few months of the outbreak at least, people continued to observe the custom of gathering at the home of the deceased with friends and neighbors to pay respects. Some relatives also showed up quite promptly in case there were any matters of inheritance that might need to be attended to.

- Eventually, people saw the writing on the wall, and many fled from infected towns in a pattern that we've seen repeated all over plague-stricken areas. But in Scandinavia, when they did flee, they tended to go en masse, as a community, rather than in family units or small groups. They were fleeing the place in which plague had broken out, but they were not actually fleeing the cause—indeed, they were bringing it with them.

- One well-known account relates how a large group of people from Bergen fled into the mountains to a place called Tusededal, where they started to build a new settlement for themselves. Unfortunately, the plague had hitched a ride with them, and within a short while, everyone who had fled to the new community died—with the exception of one girl.

- According to tradition, these facts only came to light some years later, when visitors to the area encountered this girl running wild. Although she seems to have been quite feral at first, she was eventually re-domesticated and married into a good family. She was given the name Rype, which means "wild bird."

- As the last survivor of this community established in the mountains, she was the sole inheritor of all that land. According to plague expert Philip Ziegler, for centuries after the Black Death the Rype family was one of the largest landholders in the area, proudly tracing their claim on this territory back to the days of the Great Pestilence.

LORE AND SACRIFICE

- The Black Death in Scandinavia produced a very particular kind of folklore and mythos. In Norway and Sweden, these legends tend to take the form of stories about a single surviving old man or woman, who sometimes becomes the anthropomorphized embodiment of the plague itself. Or in other cases, the stories are about lone survivors who light fires or ring bells in an attempt to find other survivors.

- Some characters become literal embodiments of the plague. In a folktale from Sweden, we have an account of an old woman who carries the plague from place to place. If she swept in front of a house's door, everyone inside would die, but if she knocked on the door with her broomstick, then only one person would die per knock, perhaps sparing some.

- In some versions of this legend, the so-called plague hag is accompanied by an old man, and he, too, has an implement that identifies him: "When he went forth with his shovel, some people were spared; but where she went forth with her broom, not even a mother's child was left alive."

- Sometimes the old man and woman are actually children. In one version from Sweden, we hear that "the plague first came as a girl with a broom (there death cleaned house) and a boy with a shovel (where he came, some people remained alive)."

- Many scholars believe that the stories about children wandering around and bringing plague with them may have some basis in reality. Given the high death rates—Scandinavia certainly matched the rest of Europe in terms of plague mortality of around 50 percent—there were certain to be plenty of orphans who had no choice but to wander the countryside, begging.

- In lore from Norway and Sweden, we almost always see the plague described as a person or people wandering through the land, bringing death and disease with them. This doesn't happen so much in Denmark, where the plague is most often associated with a mist. This may have something in common with the standard European medical theory about infected air or miasma being the source of plague. However, the scholar Timothy Tangherlini contends that this preference for one form of folktale over another is because of the "suitability of the landscape" in Demark: The rugged Norwegian landscape was unsuitable for a rolling mist, but the open Denmark lands were.

- Perhaps the most horrible thing that happened when the plague struck Scandinavia was a temporary return in some places to human sacrifice in an attempt to appease the plague. One account tells of two live children buried in the ground at a town called Gravamala; another tells of diggers asking a girl to get in a grave to test its depth, then burying her. Timothy Tangherlini cites both of these as plague legends, but a number of other scholars concede that such things may indeed have actually taken place in some instances.

- One reason that the Scandinavian reaction to the plague is seemingly so different from that we see in places like England or the main part of the European continent is that Scandinavia took longer to be Christianized, and even after it was "officially" Christian, in many places this was only nominally the case. The pagan folk traditions continued to exist and persist well into at least the 13th century in many places.

QUESTIONS TO CONSIDER

1. Why do you think the response in Norway, Sweden, and Denmark was so different—especially in terms of folklore—than what we see in the rest of Western Europe?

2. Do you see the scenario of live burials as plague appeasement as in some ways similar to the cases of abandonment of family and neighbors so familiar to us from accounts in Italy and France, or as part of the same phenomenon, with only a degree of difference, rather than kind?

SUGGESTED READING

Benedictow, *The Black Death and Later Plague Epidemics in the Nordic Countries.*

Tangherlini, "Ships, Fogs, and Traveling Pairs."

THE END OF THE FIRST WAVE

I n 1353, the first wave of the plague burned itself out. While the plague would return again and again to the European world at least once or twice a generation, from 1353 onward its virulence was greatly diminished. But that first wave was incredibly devastating. By our best estimates, the medieval world had a population of around 150 million in 1346. Seven years later, the population had dropped to around 70–75 million. This lecture looks at some unique aspects of the responses to the last gasp of the Black Death as it completed its first deadly pass through the medieval world.

BLACK DEATH TIMELINE

1346	The Black Death appears on the northwest shores of the Caspian Sea
1346–1348	The Black Death pushes toward Russia and stalls
1348	Italy, Ireland, Spain, and England are hit
1350	Scotland is hit
1349–1350	The plague reaches Sweden and pushes further into Scandinavia
1350	From Scandinavia, the plague turns south through the Baltic states into present-day Germany and Austria
1351	The Black Death turns east, pushing into Poland
1352	The Black Death reaches Russian territories from Kiev in the south and up the Dnieper River
1353	The plague arrives in Moscow and Novgorod in 1353, ending up almost back where it began
1353	The first wave burns out

ATROCITIES

- As the Black Death completed its first deadly pass through the medieval world, most people were well aware that the plague was coming. This knowledge led some desperate people to take preemptive action, and to be willing to believe all kinds of rumors and conspiracy theories.

- The most infamous was the popular belief that the Jews were causing the illness by poisoning the wells of various towns. In a series of horrifying atrocities, several communities, like Strasbourg and Bern, executed or expelled a large portion of their Jewish community before the plague had even reached their town.

- This particular brand of anti-Semitism didn't tend to recur, however, since even though all their Jews were exiled or dead, these towns still were some of the hardest hit by the plague, and there was no one left to serve as a scapegoat when the Great Mortality made its appearance.

THE BLACK DEATH IN RUSSIA

- Russian chroniclers were fully aware of the epidemic raging to the south of them as early as 1348 or 1349, but they didn't really feel its impact until 1353. The best reason for the lag scholars can figure was that the Russian steppe was thinly populated. Additionally, the presence of the dreaded Mongol Golden Horde to the south meant that no one was really inclined to move in that direction.

- In what we think of today as Russia, the effects of the Black Death at first seem to be similar to what we find in the European West—the people hardest hit were the aristocracy, who might have all kinds of land, but a shortage of bodies to work it.

- For help, Russia looked to the ruling elite in Moscow, whereas the towns and villages in most of England and places like Florence sought to cope with their community's problems on their own. Many aristocrats fled to Moscow itself. Moscow was not quite powerful enough to cope successfully with the extreme social and economic pressures the Black Death brought with it.

- Monastic houses in many parts of Russia started to gobble up all this unclaimed land that was suddenly available because the owner and all of his heirs were dead or had fled to Moscow. These vacant lands that got snapped up and consolidated became known as *pustoshi*. They became very important economic and trading centers, and soon, they began to pose real competition and a problem for independent merchants and traders who had survived the plague.

THE MONGOLS

- Prior to the arrival of the Black Death, Russia had had to deal with a series of invasions by the Mongols. From 1237–40, Mongol armies had swept out of the east and established their rule over several Russian territories.

- They completely devastated the principality of Kiev. Most of the other Russian principalities had become subject territories of the Golden Horde, having to pay taxes, supply able-bodied men for military service, and so on. A few territories in the west had elected to make themselves subject to the newly developed state of Lithuania, and thus escaped the yoke of Mongol rule.

- Thanks to the khan Oz Beg, when his replacement Jani Beg Khan came to the throne in 1342, Islam was the official state religion of the Mongols. Jani Beg was preoccupied with getting Christian merchants out of the territories near the Black Sea that were controlled by the Mongols.

- Most of these Christian merchants were Italian; they were represented in particular by the Genoese, who had long-established trading posts and fortifications along the Black Sea and in Crimea including the infamous city of Caffa.

- In 1343, the Genoese merchants fled from their trading center of Tana to the fortified city of Caffa. Jani Beg and his forces then laid siege to it.

During that siege, the plague found its way into the Mongol ranks, and then in 1346 it supposedly found its way into the city of Caffa when Jani Beg launched the corpses of plague victims into the city via trebuchet. The Genoese fled back to Genoa, stopping off in the port of Messina in Sicily on the way. The rest is history.

- The great irony here is that it was the appearance of the Black Death among the Mongols in 1346 that finally gave Russia's political and social systems a chance to recover from over a century of Mongol rule.

- By 1353, a sense of normalcy and a stable population with a reliable supply of craftsmen and laborers was just starting to get itself back in place in most of Russia. But then along came the Black Death again. The reappearance of the plague in Russia dealt the struggling labor, economic, and political systems another serious blow that would have repercussions for centuries.

- So desperate were towns and monastic communities for skilled artisans that they tightened their grip and used their power and influence to more or less enslave workers. Given that the monasteries were the ones snapping up all the free land that was available after this demographic plunge, it's not a surprise that in post-plague Russia, the Church became one of the biggest de facto slave-holding entities.

THE ONE-DAY VOTIVE CHURCH

- In many parts of Russia, there was a psychosocial plague response called the *one-day votive church*. Although these are documented as being constructed during outbreaks of plague that were slightly later than the initial wave of the mid-14th century, they're worth mentioning because they're so interesting.

- As was the case in every other country or community that was hit with plague, the losses in Russia were devastating. From Russia we get the by-now familiar stories of plague sparing no one, whether peasant or noble.

- The archbishop of Novgorod was called upon by the citizens of Pskov to come to their community and perform some religious services in the hope that this might appease God. The archbishop granted their request, traveled to Pskov, performed the services, and then died of the plague on his way back to Novgorod. And it was all for naught, as the plague continued to rage in Pskov.

- Most of the ruling elite in Moscow also succumbed, which in the short term appeared to cause a serious destabilization of the political infrastructure. Mass graves became the norm, as there was no time to give all the victims a proper burial.

- Having tried everything else, many Russian communities came together and decided that they would build structures that have come to be called *obydennye khramy*. Although there was clearly a religious impulse behind their building, it was usually the secular community leaders who organized the building effort.

- We have documentation that at least 19 of these wooden structures were built—most of them in Pskov and Novgorod, with a few in Moscow and some in other cities. They were all constructed within the span of 24 hours with communal labor. The site had to have never been used for a building before, and all the materials had to be new.

- The idea of performing a remarkable feat in a single day is attested in much of the folklore tradition of Eastern Slavic peoples, and this is probably the source of this impulse. There would be no pause in the labor—it had to be continuous, all day long, with no breaks. Certainly some of the individual laborers might pause for food or to rest for a bit, but the labor focused on the votive church itself could not stop.

- The idea here was that the continuous activity prevented Satan and other demons from finding a way in to contaminate the holy structure. As long as pious people labored on it without pause, Satan was held at bay. Then, when it was completed, there was no way for him to access it or defile it, because consecration would happen immediately.

- Building these sites remained fairly popular up until the 16th century or so. Examining the popularity of constructing these one-day votive churches offers a fascinating window into the psyches of the common people, who, because they were mostly illiterate, were unable to give us a sense of their reaction to Black Death via words. These were mostly peasants who labored with their hands, and it seems fitting that they would respond to the threat of death in a fashion similar to how they had made their living.

THE END

- With the end of 1353 came an end to the second pandemic of plague. The first had been the Plague of Justinian, in the late 6th century; the third pandemic would be in India and China at the very end of the 19th century.

- Of the three, the second, which struck the medieval world with full force between the years of 1346 and 1353, was by far the most destructive event that recorded history had ever seen.

- The plague would return continually every decade or so, sometimes striking this area or that population—old or young, sickly or healthy—more than others. But the world would never again see anything like the plague at its worst, which was between 1348 and 1350.

- The Spanish influenza epidemic of 1918, with a death toll of around 500 million worldwide, sounds like it far exceeds the death toll of the plague—but remember, we have to think in terms of population percentages.

- The Spanish flu is considered staggeringly devastating because it killed between 3–5 percent of the world's population. Consider this, though: During its peak in the UK, for every 1,000 people there were 25 deaths. Now think of the Black Death: For every 1,000 people there were 500 deaths. There is no comparison.

QUESTIONS TO CONSIDER

1. How does knowing about the Russian experience of the Black Death affect your thinking about how people reacted to the pandemic throughout Western Europe?

2. What lessons can we take away from the fact that the Black Death seemed to make a circle or noose in its progress, ending up almost back where it had first erupted?

SUGGESTED READING

Langer, "Plague and the Russian Countryside."

Zguta, "The One-Day Votive Church."

MEDIEVAL THEORIES ABOUT THE BLACK DEATH

When the Black Death devastated the medieval world in the middle of the 14th century, there arose a desperate desire to understand just what was going on. The greatest minds of the day turned their attention to figuring out the Black Death, and in the years immediately following the first outbreak in the West in 1348, dozens of plague treatises were composed and circulated. At a time when the theory of germ transmission did not yet exist and there were no antibiotics, there was little written that was of any real help. But looking at these medical and scientific theories offers a fascinating view of the medieval world.

THE UNIVERSITY OF PARIS

- The most authoritative commentary on the plague came from the medical faculty at the University of Paris, who were charged by the French king, Philip VI, with coming up with an explanation for the crisis that was confronting medieval society.

- The text is quite long, and it has two parts. In the first section, the medical faculty offers three chapters that detail the causes of the plague. In part two, they spend seven chapters offering suggestions for remedies or steps one might take in the hope of having of some effect on the plague.

- They start their tract with the general, and then get a little more specific. They go to astrology for one explanation: "We say that the distant and first cause of this pestilence was and is the configuration of the heavens." They note that on March 20th, 1345, there was a conjunction of three planets in Aquarius—Mars, Jupiter, and Saturn—which somehow caused "a deadly corruption of the air around us."

- They cite no less an authority than Aristotle, plus earlier medieval philosophers such as Albertus Magnus, who had argued that:

  > [T]he conjunction of Mars and Jupiter causes a great pestilence in the air, especially when they come together in a hot, wet sign …. For Jupiter, being wet and hot, draws up evil vapors from the earth and Mars, because it is immoderately hot and dry, then ignites the vapors, and as a result there were lightnings, sparks, noxious vapors, and fires throughout the air.

- They go on to say that the effects of this are only intensified because Mars was in the sign of Leo just before the key period in question. Though astrology is more horoscope fodder than science, in the Middle Ages, it held great significance. Indeed, in the medieval educational system, one of the seven liberal arts was astronomy, and in the Middle Ages this included within it the study of astrology.

- In astrology, different astrological signs are associated with certain assigned qualities, not unlike the idea of the four humors that were assigned to the human body. And like the use of astrology, the theory of the four humors also was of great importance as medieval people tried to figure out how to deal with the plague most effectively.

- In medieval medicine, which was based on the theories of the Greek physician Galen, the balance of the humors in the body determined basic health. The humors were considered the four main substances that regulated everything the body did. Blood was associated with air, phlegm with water, yellow bile with fire, and black bile with earth.

- The humors were also connected to ideas about appearance and personality types. In turn, based on your personality type, or dominant humor, a certain course of treatment for disease might be prescribed for you that would be different from the course prescribed for someone else who was suffering from the same affliction but who had a different dominant humor.

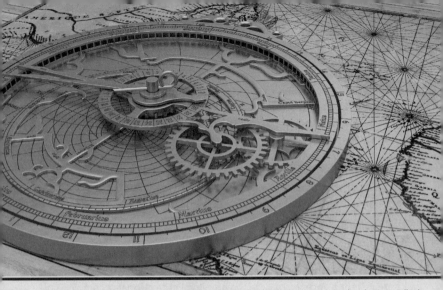

During the time of the plague, many scientists and scholars consulted a device called an astrolabe to try to get a handle on what was happening in the heavens.

- For example, if you had too much blood—or, in medieval medical terms, you were too *sanguine*—your physician might actually perform bloodletting on you to try and bring your humors "back into balance."

- Oxford scholar Geoffrey de Meaux wrote his own plague treatise on the conjunction of the planets in 1345, but he said the Paris medical faculty is wrong to focus on Jupiter as being a contributor. It was really Mars and Saturn that were cause for concern. Geoffrey asserted that eclipses played a role in the current outbreak.

THE NEAR CAUSE

- Writers also felt compelled to identify what they called the *near cause*, or the immediate cause, of plague on earth. While the primary cause is the bad air produced on earth by this conjunction of planets in an air and a fire sign, according to the medical faculty at the University of Paris, the near cause is that the pure air everyone breathes gets infected by these "noxious vapors" and spread about through gusts of wind.

- The Paris medical faculty suggested poisonous air from places like swamps, lakes, and unburied or unburned corpses probably contributed to the epidemic.

- Another factor: having corpses lying around was not conducive to the continued health of the population. This is why there were so many mass graves during the plague.

EARTHQUAKES AND WEATHER

- Some scholars of the day completely discounted the eclipse/planetary conjunction explanation. In fact, the Paris medical faculty added that in addition to the planetary issue, earthquakes could be to blame.

- The anonymous chronicler notes that "it is a matter of scientific fact" that earthquakes are caused when noxious fumes build up inside the earth and finally burst out. Furthermore, there was an earthquake in Germany on St. Paul's day in 1347, and after this, numerous people began to die from exposure to these vapors and fumes, which were then spread by storms and wind and lightning.

- While medieval experts disagreed on the source, they did agree on the fact that there was some sort of "bad air" that served as the means by which the infection was transmitted. They even came up with a name for it, which we still use today: miasma.

THE WEATHER

- Making the outbreak and the spread of miasma that much worse, according to almost every expert, was the fact that for the last few years, the weather across Europe had been unpredictable and extremely wet.

- Unusual weather patterns seem to have been the initial cause in Asia, when climate shifts caused the black rat population to move out of its traditional habitat and come into greater contact with human populations.

- The weather also probably played a role in that the winters leading up to the plague outbreak were unusually warm, as the Paris medical faculty observed. The black rat flea usually goes into hibernation in the winter, but if the weather was unseasonably warm, some of the fleas might not have hibernated, which means that what we might call "infection season" was extended.

- Of course, the idea that "infected air" from unburied corpses might be a contributing factor was absolutely correct.

AVOIDING THE PLAGUE

- The Paris medical faculty and the other scholars who weighed in on the plague didn't offer much in the way of optimism about avoiding the Great Pestilence. Here again, they turned to the theory of the four humors to explain their reasoning. "Hot and moist" bodies were particularly vulnerable, but those who were mostly dry in their humors might survive.

- We know that around 18–20 percent of those who came down with the bubonic form survived, but almost no one who contracted the pneumonic or septicemic form had a shot at beating the disease. Given the statistics, it's not much of a surprise that any medical advice about actual treatment tends to focus on the buboes.

- A scholar named John of Burgundy offered just such advice in his treatise written around 1365—so after the first wave and then a couple of subsequent smaller ones had made their way through the medieval world—and he describes his treatments with the full confidence of someone who has managed to cure many of his patients.

- He advises:
  - First, examine the buboes and figure out which organ is trying to expel the poison (heart, liver, or brain).

▸ Blood driven to the armpits indicates the heart is at play, and "blood should be let immediately from the cardiac vein, but on the same side of the body."

▸ He goes on: "[I]f the liver expels matter to the groin, and it becomes visible next to the privy member towards the inside of the leg, then a vein should be opened in the foot on the same side of the body, between the big toe and the toe next to it."

▸ Finally, "If the poison appears at the emunctories of the brain, let blood from the cephalic vein above the median vein in the arm on the same side of the body."

● Next, a medicinal mixture should be administered to the patient, with some variation depending on the infected person's humors.

● The buboes or tumors should also be treated directly. Many medieval physicians lanced the buboes, on the logical assumption that they must be the site of concentrated poison in the body. Some accounts indicate that a foul-smelling pus emerged from these lanced buboes, and the stench was so bad that other people in the room often vomited.

COUNTERING THE AIR

● One theory went that good smells could counter infected air, hence the reference to the "pocket full of posies" in the children's rhyme. Another went that bad air could counter other bad air, hence the weird spectacle of people deliberately seeking out public latrines and gathering around them to inhale deeply.

● Neither the good-smell approach nor the bad-smell approach had any real effect on the plague, but in an attempt to make the good-smell approach work, plague doctors hit upon an idea for a kind of medieval hazmat suit that probably accidentally offered some protection against plague.

● The earliest full-scale drawing we have of a plague doctor's costume comes from the 17th century, but we do have references from the 14th century to the fact that the plague doctors looked like "beaked birds." We can be reasonably sure the later drawing reflects the 14th-century costume's most important detail: the mask. The doctor could fill the mask's long beak with flowers or herbs or spices, then strap it onto his face so that he could have the benefit of the good air while keeping his hands free.

- In the early days, there was probably just a simple cutout for the eyes, but later versions seem to have actually had glass inserts there. Before he put the mask on, however, the doctor would first don something like hip-waders that would be used in fishing today. Over that, he would fasten a long coat. He'd complete the look with some gloves and boots. All of the material was probably made of some kind of oiled leather that was infused with more sweet-smelling herbs and spices.

- He would be easily identifiable by the fact that he carried a long pole, which served many purposes. It could be used to remove or set aside the clothing of the infected, and it could also be used to disperse people or push them out of the way. A broad-brimmed hat would top it all off, and also serve as an identifying marker for his occupation.

- For the doctor, at least, this outfit actually provided some real protection— there was a physical barrier between the physician and the fleas, or the bodily fluids of the infected person.

QUESTIONS TO CONSIDER

1. Try to imagine that you are a medieval person who knows nothing about the theory of germ transmission. Which "scientific" explanation would have made the most sense to you? Which the least?

2. The Black Death was the greatest medical disaster to ever hit the medieval world. Did the medieval scientific and medical communities learn anything beneficial from this experience? Do you see any examples in modern medicine that are comparable to the medieval response?

Suggested Reading

Byrne, *The Black Death.*

Horrox, *The Black Death.*

CULTURAL REACTIONS FROM FLAGELLATION TO HEDONISM

I n our previous lectures, we've caught some glimpses of how medieval people dealt with the arrival of the Great Pestilence. In this lecture, we're going to look a little more in depth at responses like those of the people who whipped themselves—the flagellants—and the people who decided that the Black Death was an excuse for hedonism. In exploring the wide variety of human responses to the death and destruction of the plague, we'll see some extremes of behavior.

THE FLAGELLANTS

- Perhaps the most dramatic and memorable response to the Black Death came from a group of people known as the flagellants. There had been flagellant movements in the century before the appearance of the Black Death, but most of these had flared up only briefly and then died out. With the arrival of the plague, they showed up again in force.

- When they appeared on the scene one day in 1348, one chronicler called them "a race without a head [that] aroused universal wonder by their sudden appearance in huge numbers." Although a large proportion of them seem to have hailed from what is today Germany, or the Netherlands, or the Rhineland, flagellants were found from England to Italy and everywhere in between in a sudden and seemingly spontaneous eruption of extreme faith.

- One chronicler notes: "They were called cross bearers either because they followed a cross carried before them on their travels, or because they prostrated themselves in the form of a cross during their processions." They used whips to strike themselves until "their bodies were bruised and swollen and blood rained down, spattering the wall nearby."

Flagellants

- As you may recall, medieval society was, ideally, organized into three groups—those who fight, those who pray, and those who work. The fighters protected society; the clergy prayed to alleviate sinfulness; and the workers supported the other two orders. The flagellants saw themselves as performing the work of the second—seeking to save the world with very public displays of self-punishment.

- The theory the flagellants were operating under was that because Christ was whipped before his crucifixion, those who chose to inflict this punishment on themselves were joining with Christ. To be sure, throughout the Middle Ages, many religious people sought to punish their flesh as a means of refining their souls. But the difference is, in most cases, this punishment was meant to be private.

- The most popular approach was to wear an article of clothing known as a hair shirt underneath one's outer clothing and against one's skin. The closest equivalent today would be to wear a vest of steel wool that somehow was also infected with lice and fleas. But ideally, no one besides the penitent and his confessor would know about this. Otherwise, it would be a sin of pride.

- With their very public approach to penance, the flagellants were a bit of a problem, although they attracted an impressive following when they first showed up during the initial wave of the Black Death.

FLAGELLANT TACTICS

- One chronicler relates that "when they came to cities, towns, and villages, they formed themselves into a procession, with hoods or hats pulled down over their foreheads, and sad and downcast eyes." The flagellants would process this way through the town, singing a hymn, until they reached the town's church.

- Then real show would begin. The German *Chronicon Henrici de Hervordia* gives us an exemplary description of the usual program of their behavior. According to this account, after the flagellants had entered a town, they would lock themselves in the community's church, strip themselves almost naked, and then burst out of the north doors of the church wearing only a loincloth.

- Next, they would arrange themselves on the ground in front of the various entrances to the church. Some of them might lie in the shape of a cross, but others positioned their bodies on their sides or backs or faces in some sort of physical code for the sin they were most guilty of.

- Then one of the group's members would go around and whip each of the penitents who were lying on the ground in turn, and once he was done, someone else would take over the whip, and it would begin again. It was, to say the least, a spectacle that attracted the attention of the locals.

FLAGELLANTS AND THE CHURCH

- The flagellants made an appearance in Avignon when the plague struck there, and the pope rather uneasily allowed them to practice their behavior for a very short time. But there was a pretty quick consensus on the part of most Church officials that the flagellant movement was excessive, and dangerous, and, perhaps most concerning, the participants started to think that they had a right to act as preachers. They showed contempt toward the Church's sacraments and clergy.

- Pope Clement rather swiftly issued a bull against the flagellant movement, and those who refused to submit to this correction were excommunicated. The flagellants ignored this until nobles and other elites began to side against them. Indeed, four months after Clement issued his bull, the French king got on board and condemned the movement as well, and by 1350, they were on their way to disappearing again.

PLEASURE SEEKERS

- In contrast to the flagellant movement, we have examples of people who went the other direction—figuring that if these were going to be their last days on earth, they might as well spend them doing something pleasurable. The accounts of these behaviors are less detailed and more anecdotal than what we get in the chronicle accounts of the flagellants.

- One of the most famous of these accounts comes from a fairly reliable source, Giovanni Boccaccio, who in the introduction to the *Decameron* famously detailed the horrors of the plague when it first struck Florence. He wrote of victims dropping dead in the streets, of the dead buried in mass graves, of people abandoning not only the city but also their friends and neighbors.

- But then he says: "Others … maintained that an infallible way of warding off this appalling evil was to drink heavily, enjoy life to the full, go round singing and merrymaking, gratify all of one's cravings whenever the opportunity offered, and shrug the whole thing off as one enormous joke."

- In John of Reading's chronicle account of a later outbreak of plague in 1361, we see signs that, in John's eyes at least, the social order was completely breaking down: "This year the mortality was particularly of males .... However, the greatest cause of grief was provided by the behavior of the women." He goes on to complain of adultery, incest, and fornication in general.

CHOREOMANIA

- One response to the plague seems to have been something called *choreomania*, in which people participated in dancing parties. We tend to see the choreomaniacs during later outbreaks—especially in the 1370s—but we can regard them as the successors to those people who gave in to hedonism during the first outbreak in the 1340s.

- This movement, like the flagellant movement, seems to have sprung up mostly in the Rhineland and Flanders, especially in the towns of Cologne, Metz, Liege, and Treves. One chronicler reports more than 500 dancers in Cologne alone. Particularly scandalous, according to this chronicler, is that most of the women who participated in these dances were both unmarried and pregnant.

- But not everyone looked at these dancing parties and their participants with disdain; indeed, some communities, especially during later outbreaks of plague, would actually organize dances for the whole town. In some instances, these dances were supposedly meant to act as some sort of force that would keep the plague at bay.

- One story tells that the citizens of Basle, during a plague outbreak, would go and dance around a pine tree on a plain known as the Witch's Mead until the infection had worked its way through their community and was on to the next.

- In other communities, these dance parties were conceived of as a way of trying to lift the depression that was sure to attend an outbreak of disease. Indeed, celebratory annual dance parties that still take place to this day in many towns trace their origins back to the days of plague. In Munich, for example, there is the Schafflertanz and the Metzgersprung—celebrations held in the modern period that, according to tradition, first came into being as a response to plague.

- There are accounts as well of a general mood of licentiousness—in plenty of instances, people seem to have given themselves over to pleasure. The scholar Johannes Nohl cites one particular instance in Paris during a plague outbreak, of which an anonymous chronicler writes:

    Without heed of what is decent or indecent the people live only guided by their own instincts, and do by day or night, alone or in company, whatever their inclination may prompt them. And it is not only the laity that behave thus, but the nuns in the convents also, neglecting their rules, abandon themselves to carnal lust, and deem that by voluptuousness and excess they will prolong their lives.

- Again, these accounts of dancing and licentiousness are not as detailed or as convincing as the accounts we see about the other extreme—the flagellants, and, to a lesser degree, a general increase in religiosity.

REACTIONS

- Still, there are some clues about the proliferation of naughty behavior. For example, in the midst of serious outbreaks in the Italian city of Florence and the town of Tournai in what is present-day Belgium, a slew of "moral legislation" was passed.

- These laws strictly forbade or put limits on activities like prostitution and gambling. But it might not be the case that there was a sudden uptick in prostitution and gambling activities in these and other cities in the face of the Great Mortality.

- What's more likely is that, when confronted with the Black Death, the city leaders, most likely being Christian believers, were trying to curtail every sin they could, so as to atone before God.

- The most horrifying reaction to the Black Death was, without question, the widespread pogroms against the Jewish communities. Many people were desperate to find someone—anyone—to blame for the misery and death raining down upon them.

- Jewish communities, which were usually isolated or ghettoized in relationship to a major town and whose members were limited to certain undesirable professions, were the target of hysteria that swept through much of Europe from 1348 to 1350.

QUESTIONS TO CONSIDER

1. How do you think you and people in your community might react when confronted with a threat like plague? Would your reactions be similar to the variety of responses we saw in mid-14th century? Why or why not?

2. Are there any responses to natural disasters or epidemics in the modern world that seem of a piece with the flagellant movement? Or is that mentality unique to the medieval world, do you think?

SUGGESTED READING

Aberth, *From the Brink of Apocalypse.*

Byrne, *Daily Life During the Black Death.*

JEWISH PERSECUTION DURING THE BLACK DEATH

T he arrival of the plague in medieval Europe marked the beginning of one of the most devastating events humanity had ever experienced. In the face of an implacable and unstoppable enemy for which there seemed no defense and no cure, people responded in just about every way you can imagine. Some people engaged in denial, some turned to religion, and some decided to party. But others looked for someone to blame—and they found their scapegoat in the Jewish communities that existed throughout the medieval world.

ANTI-SEMITISM

- Jewish communities existed throughout the medieval world for centuries—for example, they had been in what is today Spain, on the Iberian Peninsula, since as early as the second century. Trading hubs like Sicily had also long had a diverse population that included Jews.

- Around the year 1000, the population of the medieval world was around 75 million people. At that time there was a warming period, known as the Little Climatic Optimum, which made food more abundant by lengthening growing seasons. The climate shift made fishing waters off the British coast and in the North Sea more productive. Advances in farming technology also meant that crop yields were even higher.

- All of this put together meant that suddenly there was a population boom. By the 12th century, good, arable land was becoming scarce, and, as human beings have done since time immemorial, people sought to protect their own families first, and then those with whom they identified with on a broader level.

- Starting in the 12th century, this led to what historian R. I. Moore has called "the formation of a persecuting society." Marginal groups—like lepers, non-mainstream Christians, heretics, women, and people whose sexuality was not considered heteronormative—were now even further marginalized. The biggest marginalized group was the Jews.

- Suddenly, a whole crop of regulations came into being that essentially took the right to farm or engage in certain other trades and crafts away from the Jews and gave them the right to practice only least preferred trades in medieval society, for example, moneylending.

- Also starting around the 12th century, many Jewish communities now had restrictions on where they lived—in many places they were "ghettoized" into a Jewish quarter that usually had some sort of curfew. That was often actually walled off from the main community to which it was attached.

- The French King Philip II expelled the Jews from Paris in 1182 but then after confiscating their property, brought some of them back on the condition that they work exclusively for him as his bankers. King Edward I expelled the Jews altogether from England in 1290.

- Add to that the crusading fervor that swept Europe when, in 1095, Pope Urban II called for Christian forces to head to the Middle East and retake Jerusalem and the rest of the Holy Land from the Muslim rulers who controlled it. Several of the crusaders, on their way overland through Europe, got to the area of the Rhineland, which had several large Jewish populations. They decided to kill the Jews, as they were non-Christians.

SCAPEGOATING

- When the Black Death struck some two and a half centuries after the onset of crusading fervor, once again the Jews were a convenient scapegoat for a population desperately looking for some to blame.

- Some chronicles make a point of saying that the accusations that Jews were causing the plague by poisoning wells and other water sources for various towns was obviously wrong, because Jews were dying in numbers equal to the mortality rates of non-Jews.

- Other chronicles claim that in some places the Jewish population seemed relatively unaffected compared to the mainstream population. For a long time, most scholars assumed this was lie. But some have theorized that there may have been some truth to this claim, in at least a few communities. Two reasons:
  - The ghettoization of the Jews would have reduced their direct contact with the plague-infested Christian community.
  - The celebration of Passover involves getting rid of all the foodstuffs made of grain in a home—removing food for rodents. No rodents would mean no plague-carrying fleas.

- In some cases, it may actually have been the case that at least a few Jewish communities suffered fewer losses than the Christian towns to which they were connected. This, combined with the grave threat posed by the Black Death, could give rise to a violent anti-Semitic response.

PERSECUTION

- As they attempted to get to the root cause of what was causing the Great Mortality, many leaders took it upon themselves to round up some Jews, torture them, and then get a confession about what was happening and how they were going about it.

- For example, we have a chronicle account of a Franciscan friar named Herman Gigas, who, when he attempted to explain the origins of the Black Death, noted some said the "Jews planned to wipe out all the Christians with poison and had poisoned wells and springs everywhere. And many Jews confessed as much under torture."

- The "confession" played into the fears of an already paranoid populace by clearly suggesting that this was a well-thought-out campaign organized and run at the highest levels of the Jewish community.

- Pogroms against the Jews continued to spread, mostly throughout the German-speaking lands—from present-day Austria to the Netherlands, including present-day Switzerland and Germany. Pogroms also took place in parts of what is today considered France and Spain.

- Once the persecution had started in 1348, it continued well into 1349. The means of execution were truly shocking. For example, in the town of Basel, special wooden houses were constructed; the Jews of the community were shut up inside them, and then they were set on fire.

WATERSHED MOMENTS

- Three moments are key to understanding how the pogroms came to be. The first is the famous "confession" of Jews in region of Savoy. The main confession supposedly came from a man named Balavigny, who, after several days of torture, admitted not only to poisoning wells, but to it being part of an international Jewish conspiracy. His confession was blatantly false; for example, he claimed the poison came from a basilisk, a mythical creature. Nonetheless, news of his confession spread through letters.

- The second watershed moment in Jewish persecution involved the citizens of Strasbourg. Here, leaders filled in wells or had their buckets destroyed. Then, even though the plague had not yet reached Strasbourg, on February 14, 1349, all of the Jews of the community were rounded up and executed in a process that took almost a week.
  - Many of the leaders of Strasbourg had previously sought to protect the Jews in their community. The mayor and several of the most prominent burghers of the town tried to enforce an order of protection for the Jewish population.
  - These leaders came into conflict with some of the most powerful guild leaders of the community—in particular, the butchers' guild. In the

Strasbourg massacre

face of this opposition, most of the burghers gave up their leadership positions.

- For a time, the mayor, Peter Swarber, stood alone against them, but then he, too, was forced to resign his position. Almost immediately, a new council was selected, and the day after its members were sworn in, all the Jews in the community were rounded up and made ready for execution.

- Some other Christian leaders tried to protect the Jewish communities in their areas as well. For example, Duke Albrecht of Austria issued an order of protection when the pogroms started, but by 1349, the anti-Semitic hysteria had increased to such a degree that he withdrew his protection.

- One chronicler relates that some high-ranking citizens no longer wished to offer support to the Jewish community:

> But the imperial citizens did not want to go on supporting them … and so they wrote to Duke Albrecht of Austria, who was protecting his Jewish subjects in the counties of Pfirt,

Alsace, and Kyburg, and told him that either he had them burnt by his own judges or they would burn them themselves. So the Duke ordered them to be burnt by his own judges, and they were finally burnt on 18 September.

- The third major event—the horrifying climax of anti-Semitic action during the Black Death—occurred in the German town of Cologne. Cologne at first held out for a long time as a place whose Jews were protected.

- For many people, the desire to protect the Jews may have had more to do with maintaining a stable social and economic order rather than making a stand against injustice. In any case, because Cologne had been one of the more reasonable communities, many Jews fled there in the face of persecution in their home cities and towns.

- This explosion in the Jewish population of Cologne finally began to worry its Christian citizens, the more paranoid of whom began to imagine that the Jews were gathering in a sizeable force in Cologne the better to take over and defeat the Christians there.

- The leaders of the Jewish community got wind of this growing dissatisfaction and began to take precautions—retreating within the ghetto and distributing weapons among the residents. These weapons were probably not the Jews', but were most likely collateral that Christian money borrowers had left to secure a loan.

- A small group of Christians acted as spies, pretending that they were on the side of the Jews and wanted to join their resistance against the Christians of Cologne. Once inside, they learned that the Jews were planning a raid on a particular quarter of Cologne on a particular day—most likely because they were running out of supplies, and not because they had any desire to "conquer" Cologne.

- The spies alerted the leaders outside the ghetto, and when the Jewish contingent made their move, they found an army waiting for them. What happened next was a remarkable thing: a huge pitched battle in the middle of a major city. Although many Christians died, it was the Jews who sustained the largest losses, with some reports saying that 25,000 were killed in the fighting.

THE AFTERMATH

- It's estimated that in German-speaking countries alone approximately 340 towns launched pogroms against their Jewish populations. Scholars estimate that by the time the dust had settled, 80 Jewish communities were wiped off the map completely. This doesn't even take into account the numerous anti-Semitic activities in France and Spain that we know were also happening.

- But once the first wave of plague receded, so too did the hysterical anti-Semitism. Many of the Jewish citizens who had fled the pogroms—heading to places like Vienna—were invited to resettle in their hometowns within a decade of the first wave of plague.

- By late 1350, several chroniclers—and even Pope Clement VI himself—started to voice the observation that the Jews seemed to be dying in numbers as great as Christians. And more to the point, the plague struck hardest in precisely those towns that had already expelled or executed all their Jews. Strasbourg murdered its Jews in February 1349; just a few months later, in July of that same year, the plague struck there with great ferocity.

- All of this together took the power out of the idea that Jews were somehow responsible for the Black Death, and indeed, on a few occasions during future outbreaks, Jewish and Christian leaders would join together to offer prayers for deliverance from the plague.

QUESTIONS TO CONSIDER

1. The trumped-up "confessions" of Jews who were tortured into admitting to well poisoning are remarkable in many respects, not the least of which is the very specific description of the poison. Do you think these descriptions made the accusations more or less believable to a medieval mind? What effect does it have on a modern mind?

2. Are there any glimmers of hope for humanity in the description of the medieval persecutions of the Jews, both during the Black Death and on other occasions?

SUGGESTED READING

Aberth, *From the Brink of Apocalypse.*

Byrne, *Encyclopedia of the Black Death.*

PLAGUE'S EFFECTS ON THE MEDIEVAL CHURCH

D uring the time of the Black Death, the Church is everywhere. It was part of every element of the medieval infrastructure. It imbued and influenced politics, economics, family relationships, scholarly study, friendships, social structures, military conflicts, territorial disputes … the list goes on and on. Thus, when the plague struck the medieval world in late 1347, it was completely natural that people would turn to the Church for guidance, answers, deliverance, and comfort. In general, the Church sought to respond as effectively as possible—but in the face of such a pandemic with no known treatment or cure, that effectiveness was severely limited.

THE CHURCH

- In the medieval world in the West, there was no *Catholic* Church. There was only the Church. It was at least 1,500 years after Christ's death that Christian belief systems like those of Luther and Calvin developed out of and distinguished themselves from what we call Catholicism today.

- When the plague first erupted on the scene, the initial approach taken by Church leaders was to use this horrible event as an opportunity to remind humanity of the grievous nature of their sins. Sermon after sermon described how God had sent the Great Pestilence to teach humankind a lesson.

- There was also an attempt to appease God: Pope Clement VI himself composed a special Mass in response to the outbreak of plague, in which he appealed to God for forgiveness and mercy.

- The archbishop of York, William Zouche, also offered an official response to the plague. In a letter dated July 28, 1348—so right around the moment the plague first showed up in England—Zouche ordered that the parishes of England should have devout processions and special prayers.

- King Edward III of England asked the Archbishop of Canterbury, John de Stratford, to arrange for prayers to be said against the plague throughout the parishes in the environs of Canterbury. Stratford, unfortunately, died of plague before he could comply.
  - The responsibility was handed off to the prior of Christchurch in Canterbury, and he composed a letter to the bishop of London in which he asked for help in conveying the royal request to other bishops in the realm.
  - The letter is remarkable for many reasons, not least of which is the lengthy discussion of the evils and sins that the people of England must have committed for God to rain down this affliction upon them.
  - Toward the end, the prior writes, "… you should arrange to grant indulgences to every one of your flock undertaking the things specified above. You should also … tell all the other bishops to add indulgences on their own account, as seems best to them."

- Indulgences had first become a really key part of the Western Christian belief system during the Crusades. At that time, the Church called on soldiers to retake the holy city of Jerusalem and surrounding regions, and offered them full indulgences if they participated and died while on campaign. In other words, as bad as some of the Western warriors might have been in their lives, if they took up the cross and marched on the Holy Land, they got to go straight to heaven and skip purgatory altogether.

- But none of these things had any effect on the Black Death. It wasn't too long before people had had enough. As Philip Ziegler puts it: "All that the Church had done was wait until it was too late and then point out to their flock how wicked they had been."

THE CLERGY
- In the first wave of plague, we have evidence that any number of clergymen sought to do their best to comfort their dying parishioners. The outcome of this was that most of these good, sincere clergymen died. Those that remained alive sometimes abandoned their posts out of fear of contracting plague.

- Since the plague seemed to affect the clergy in equal if not greater numbers than the general population, the institution of the Church, just like every other organization, started to suffer from a serious shortage of manpower.

- This meant that suddenly the life of cleric or monk or priest—a highly desirable, stable, secure life that that had heretofore been available almost exclusively to members of the nobility—was now open to almost anyone alive and breathing.

- While this sudden fluidity and mobility was an unexpected boon for many individuals, it was not such a good thing for the Church. In the immediate wake of the plague, all rules of religious ordination were more or less abandoned.

- England provides a clear example of this. In Winchester in 1349 and 1350, records tell us, 27 new members of the clergy were ordained subdeacons, then deacons, and then priests all in the space of a few days—rather than the several years this advancement would normally have taken. They then got sent out to their parishes and Church offices with almost zero experience.

- The Church was taking everyone it could, and the result was a flood of ill-qualified and unprepared priests who were supposed to minister to a flock that was in desperate need of informed and sincere religious guidance. Clearly, they weren't going to be getting it, and this caused the reputation of the Church to fall still further in the eyes of the general population.

- Far from being experts on matters scriptural or religious, the new crop of priests were often illiterate, and they were poorly suited in terms of temperament for the job they were now supposed to do. It was not sincere belief or faith that had led most of them to seek out ordination but rather the promise of a secure living.

- It had long been the case that in extreme circumstances any baptized Christian could perform necessary rites—midwives, in particular, very often had to perform the rite of baptism if they delivered a child who seemed likely to die before a priest could be summoned. But the fact that the bishop announced to his parishioners that they should go ahead and make confession to whoever happened to be present is a clear indication that things were extremely dire.

- While many of these ecclesiastical vacancies came about because a priest died, others existed because some higher-ranking priest had died and a lower-ranking official saw the chance to jump up the ladder of clerical advancement. Because most ecclesiastical offices came with a stipend of some kind, and because there was a desperate need to fill them, many of the ordained started asking for the stipends to be increased.

- The archbishop of Canterbury, seeking to curb this, issued an injunction against it—right around the time the secular government in England passed the Statute of Laborers, which fixed wages for laborers at pre-plague levels and put restrictions on movement.

THE MENDICANTS

- At the same time that established institutions like monasteries and the office of the parish priest were suffering, a relatively new arm of the Church was gaining credibility and popularity. This order, the mendicants, operated somewhat outside the Church's main conventions, and their actions during the Black Death would ironically further erode the authority of the establishment they were supposedly a part of.

- For most of its history, the Church's officials, especially monks, had to conform to certain rules of behavior. In addition to poverty, most monks and some other Church officials vowed to observe "stability of place," meaning they were to stay in their monastery or secure in their parish offices.

- But then in 1215, at the Fourth Lateran Council, a new reform monastic movement was given license. This was the Friars Minor, one of the first mendicant movements, as founded by St. Francis of Assisi. Francis had famously argued that to have a truly Christological experience, monks should rid themselves of all possessions and throw themselves on the mercy of the world.

St. Francis of Assisi

- *Mendicant* means "begging," and when these orders were approved, there was much grumbling among those who thought that stable, established houses of God were the way to go. The countergument was that these monasteries had become places of too much comfort and even luxury to produce and maintain truly holy men.

- In the beginning, at least, the mendicants didn't have a motherhouse they could return to. They were out in the world in a sincere attempt to save it. And when the Black Death started ravaging the countryside, a potential savior from outside looked like a very attractive option for those who were living in fear.

- Survivors had been seeing their regular parish priests having no effect on the plague, contracting it and dying themselves, abandoning their posts entirely, or demonstrating fear of the plague. Into this came the friars. It certainly would have been striking to a community when a devout holy man wandered in from the outside and willingly took on the task of tending to the sick and bereft.

- While certainly the friars contracted and died from plague at the same rates as everyone else, the sincerity and devotion with which most of them approached the challenge at hand would have made a strong impression on those who would survive and later remember who it was that came to help in the darkest hour.

- While friars were officially part of the Church, they were so different from what people were accustomed to that their presence and behavior surely seemed like a challenge to the long-standing practices of the institution they were are a part of. It's no surprise that those who were members of the established ecclesiastical hierarchy saw the popularity of the mendicant orders as a threat.

- Indeed, many religious leaders signed and presented a petition to Pope Clement VI in Avignon—remember, he was sitting between his two fires for most of the epidemic. In this petition they asked that he abolish the mendicant orders, or at the very least forbid them from preaching and hearing confession. This was in 1351, after the worst of the plague had made its way through most of Western Europe, and those who had survived were attempting to get back on their feet.

- The pope's response was rather astonishing. He said:

> And if their preaching be stopped, about what can you preach to the people? If on humility, you yourselves are the proudest of the world, arrogant and given to pomp. If on poverty, you are the most grasping and the most covetous …. If on chastity—but we will be silent on this, for God knoweth what each man does and how many of you satisfy your lusts.

- Pope Clement VI was by no means a model ecclesiastic. He enjoyed all the comforts that came with his high status and was generally willing to look the other way when it came to infractions of the chastity and poverty clauses of the standard monastic oath. For him to excoriate the bishops and priests who were appealing to him to kick out the mendicants meant that the state of the Church at this point must have been corrupt indeed.

QUESTIONS TO CONSIDER

1. What is most surprising to you about official ecclesiastical responses to plague?

2. Just how badly did the plague hurt the credibility, status, and power of the Church?

SUGGESTED READING

Cohn, *The Cult of Remembrance and the Black Death*.

Dohar, *The Black Death and Pastoral Leadership*.

PLAGUE SAINTS AND POPULAR RELIGION

W hen the Black Death raced through medieval Europe, everyone was caught flat-footed—governments, individuals, traders, merchants, and of course the Church. Like almost every other institution, the Church was slow to react and ineffective when it finally did. Its inability to offer either countermeasures or comfort to those who were suffering dealt that institution a serious blow in terms of how people regarded it and whether they would continue to respect its authority. But just because people became disillusioned with the Church doesn't mean they lost their faith in general. Quite the contrary—for answers in the face of the greatest mortality the medieval world had ever seen, many people turned to faith.

CHAPELS AND HOLIDAYS

- Even as the popular estimation of the Church was at an all-time low, expressions of religious devotion increased down at the level of the man on the street. In Italy, for example, 50 more religious holidays were celebrated in the immediate aftermath of the first wave of plague, and these came about by popular acclamation rather than an official ecclesiastical pronouncement.

- Throughout the countryside of Western Europe, but most especially in England, there was a burst of construction in the form of chantry chapels. The purpose of these chapels was to serve as dedicated spaces where clergy would sing Masses for the souls of the departed.

- It was believed—and this belief was sanctioned by the Church—that those still living on earth could help lessen the time a loved one's soul spent in purgatory by saying prayers themselves, or arranging for a priest to perform Masses or say prayers on behalf of the departed. In order to guarantee this, the chantry chapel needed to be endowed—that is, the departed or his or her family needed to arrange for payment for the priest's or other clergyman's services in performing these Masses.

- This—the wealthy seemingly being able to buy their way into heaven— was exactly the kind of thing that bothered reformers like Martin Luther, who famously nailed his 95 theses to the church door at Wittenberg in 1517.

SAINTS

- When God's earthly representatives seemed both unwilling and unable to help those afflicted by plague, people turned to other intercessors for assistance. In particular, they began to pray to specific saints for special help against the plague.

- Some of these saints were considered intercessors or appropriate figures to pray to for help. The Virgin Mary had long been a popular saint for those concerned with matters of illness, as had her mother, Saint Anne.

- When plague struck the port city of Messina in Sicily, the citizens appealed to the patriarch of Catania, the highest-ranking ecclesiastical official in Sicily, to bring the relics of Saint Agatha that were kept in Catania to Messina in the hope that this would effect a miraculous cure.

- Messina's citizens resisted, so the patriarch came up with a compromise: He poured water over Agatha's relics, and then brought this now-holy water to Messina. But no great miracle came—indeed, the patriarch himself was one of the victims of the plague, as were so many Church officials.

- Other saints brought front and center included Saint Sebastian, Saint Roch, and Saint Rose of Viterbo, among many, many others. By one count, there are over 100 saints who were specifically identified as interceding in matters of plague in the wake of the first wave of the Great Pestilence.

SAINT SEBASTIAN

- Sebastian's story is quite typical of what we find among those martyred for Christianity in the early days. Sometime around the end of the 3rd century, Sebastian was a member of the Roman military. The empire at this time was still firmly pagan and polytheistic, and this new upstart Christian religion was considered dangerous and subversive.

- When Sebastian was discovered to be a Christian, he was imprisoned. While in prison he managed to convert a bunch of other people to Christianity, and then, because he refused to renounce his faith, he was executed by being tied to a post and shot full of arrows.

- Sebastian has a connection to the Great Mortality for two reasons:
  - The Roman god Mars is very often represented holding a bow, and while arrows were instruments of war, they also could spread disease.
  - According to an earlier Christian chronicler named Paul the Deacon, it was the intercession of Saint Sebastian in the year 680 that caused the end of an epidemic that had been ravaging Rome. That wave of plague might have been a very late outbreak of the Plague of Justinian.

SAINT ROCH

- As for Saint Roch, the major points of his story go something like this: He was born into a noble family in Montpellier, France, near the end of the 13th century. His parents were very religious. (Note that it's likely Roch's story is a conflation of more than one person.)

- When his parents died, Roch gave away all his possessions and set off for Rome. Upon his arrival there, he found a great illness ravaging the city. He immediately set about helping those who were ill.

- Most of his story is about dealing with illness, so Saint Roch makes a great deal of sense as a plague intercessor. He's not attested, however, until around 1391. In those accounts, we learn of a man who was very active during a confirmed outbreak of plague in Italy around 1376. This date would make much more sense, as whatever illness Roch encountered in

Saint Sebastian

the earlier version of the story in Rome in the 1320s couldn't have been bubonic plague, as it hadn't arrived on the scene yet.

- In any event, starting at the end of the 14th century, Roch became the go-to saint to pray to whenever plague shows up. Indeed, when plague broke out at the Council of Constance in 1414, the religious in leaders in attendance prayed to Roch, and supposedly the outbreak ended.

- Roch was venerated as a saint and prayed to for deliverance from the plague by thousands of people long before he was actually formally declared a saint by the institution of the Church itself.

- Saint Roch was sometimes added to a roster of "helper saints" that came into being shortly after the Black Death swept through the Rhineland. Eventually, the Church would officially recognize the Fourteen Holy Helpers, which included figures like the saints Barbara, Catherine of Alexandria, and Margaret of Antioch, who interceded in cases of fever, sudden death, and childbirth, among other things.

ROSE OF VITERBO

- Rose of Viterbo is another saint who was venerated for centuries before her official canonization. Rose was apparently a very pious child, and when she was just seven years old she began a life that would be marked by prayer, fasting, and long periods of seclusion. When she was 10, the Virgin Mary spoke to her and told her to join the religious order of Saint Francis of Assisi.

- During her lifetime she was respected not only for her pious religious devotion, but also for her ability to foretell the future, which apparently did on a number of occasions, including one instance in which she accurately predicted the death of the Holy Roman Emperor. She herself died in 1251 or 1252, peacefully, in her father's home.

- Rose didn't have much to do with the plague until the people of Viterbo were facing something like their 10th outbreak of plague. The one that

Saint Roch

struck in 1450—a century after the first wave—was particularly bad. Their desperation was such that they started scouring the records of holy people who had been associated with Viterbo at some point in the past. They found Rose, and many people began to pray to her for deliverance from the plague. The Church canonized Rose late in the 15th century.

OTHER RESPONSES

- Praying to holy men and women who would eventually become saints was hardly the only example of popular religious expression that erupted after the plague. Probably the most obvious example of a "grassroots" religious response was that of the flagellant movement, which seemed to arise in several places across the continent almost out of nowhere.

- The movement went on until their behavior became truly bizarre, with activities like trying to bring a dead child back to life. They also began preaching against Church officials. Ecclesiastical authorities moved to issue injunctions against their behavior, including a papal bull condemning flagellation as a response to the plague.

- Much more mainstream was the practice of pilgrimage. Pilgrimages had been widespread throughout the medieval world long before the plague appeared on the scene, but the plague boosted their popularity. The length varied: Pilgrims might travel to the next town over, where the church perhaps possessed some relic associated with a saint, or they might go long distances.

- One church might have a saint's eyeball, while another might have her shinbone or her cloak. It was a special thing if the body of a saint was intact at one particular location—that church was lucky indeed.

- The presence or absence of these relics could mean stability or collapse for a church that did or did not possess them. Those who came on pilgrimage could be expected to make an offering of thanks, and those offerings would go straight into the church or monastery's coffers.

- Large groups of people from all over the medieval world traveling through it and then gathering together in large groups is exactly the opposite of what people should do in the middle of a pandemic. It's a cruel irony that this attempt to avoid the plague probably infected more people with it, and probably brought it to places that had so far managed to avoid infection.

- Those pilgrims who did make it home and shared their experience all talked of roadblocks put up by members of certain communities who really didn't want a steady stream of potentially infected people marching through their town.

ROME

- Apart from Jerusalem, the greatest pilgrimage you could make during the Middle Ages was to the holy city of Rome. At the end of the 13th century, Pope Boniface VIII had declared that the year 1300 would be a jubilee year. By that, he meant that all those who made a pilgrimage to Rome that year would receive full remission of all their sins as long as they were truly contrite and fulfilled his command to visit the basilicas of Saint Peter and Saint Paul once a day for 15 days. If you were an inhabitant of Rome and didn't have the burden of traveling to the city, you could partake in the jubilee as well as long as you went to those basilicas once a day each for 30 days.

- Jubilees were originally supposed to occur every century, but Pope Clement called a jubilee for 1350. Those who had managed to survive the Black Death to this point felt a strong compulsion to travel to Rome both to give thanks and, of course, to get a ticket on the express train out of purgatory.

- Given all that traveling from far-flung locations and the injunction to gather at specific places on specific consecutive days, the plague had plenty of opportunity to find new hosts and achieve its last gasp of virulence before this first wave of the Great Mortality finally began to recede.

QUESTIONS TO CONSIDER

1. Which of the "popular" religious responses to the Black Death most interested/surprised you?

2. Do you think in the modern world we would see a similar range of faith-based responses to an epidemic, or has our society's worldview fundamentally shifted?

SUGGESTED READING

Nohl, *The Black Death.*

Williman, ed., *The Black Death.*

ARTISTIC RESPONSES TO THE BLACK DEATH

O ut of the Black Death came new and innovative forms of artistic expression. New subjects appearing in all kinds of paintings, sculptures, wood carvings, and other art forms are evidence of an attempt to cope with a serious tragedy. As we'll see in this lecture, that beauty could emerge from such a horrific experience is one of the things that has long been a hallmark of what it means to be human.

GRIM THEMES

- One very popular artistic trend was that of "the three living meet the three dead." This was part of a larger *memento mori* tradition, which translates roughly to something like: "Remember that you are going to die." This type of art, like many others, existed before the plague but became more prevalent after.

Example of the three living meeting the three dead

- In both the textual and visual versions of this story, three living men traveling on their way encounter three corpses. Most often, the three living are from the nobility and the clergy—in several instances, we see a pope, an emperor, and a king depicted. In every case, though, the message is the same: You may be alive now, but someday you'll be dead.

- Even more grim were the architectural and sculptural works known as *transi* tombs. These were somewhat similar to tombs called *gisants*, which have an effigy statue usually representing the deceased as both asleep and looking their finest. The big difference: With a *transi* tomb, the effigy is not of the deceased represented as when they looked their best and were at their most powerful. Instead, the case of the *transi* tomb, the effigy is of decaying corpse.

- More than one scholar has commented that this can arguably be seen as a reaction to the necessity of mass graves during the worst of the plague— there was something horrifying to the medieval mind about being lost to eternity in a plague pit, with no marker to note your place or any living person to point out where your earthly remains are buried. The vogue in tombs with effigies may have been a direct reaction against that horrifying anonymity.

- The most famous depiction of the mass burials that seem to have inspired this revolt comes from the 1350 manuscript of Gilles le Muisis, who was abbot at Tournai when the plague broke out. Gilles reports on proclamations made by the city officials of Tournai. These include rules about the depth of graves and injunctions against piling bodies up on top of each other, among many other things.

LEAVING TRACES

- In the face of the Great Mortality, those who could took steps to ensure that they would be remembered. Black Death scholar Joseph Byrne observes that an examination of wills from before the plague shows people making charitable bequests here and there, and the terms of the bequests are rather general.

- After the first wave of plague, Byrne notes more and more people from further down the social ladder were making these bequests, and when they did, they were careful to stipulate things like the carving of their family crest above an orphanage they were donating to.

- Byrne points to the example of the Datini family of Florence. When Francesco Datini's father died in 1348, he left a scattering of donations to various religious institutions per his will. But when Francesco made up his will, he took a completely different tack. He specified that an enormous sum should go in just one direction—to found an orphanage that would be named after him.

- When he died in 1410, his instructions were carried out, and his wife commissioned an artist to paint huge frescoes on the outside walls of their palazzo. These frescoes were all meant to represent Francesco performing numerous charitable activities. That she wanted these to adorn the outside of their grand home, where everyone passing by could see them, means that she really wanted everyone to remember her husband and their family.

Danse Macabre

- The most widespread and popular form of artistic expression to emerge from the ravages of the Black Death was the representation of the *danse macabre*, or "dance of death." The earliest use of the term that we can find comes from a Frenchman named Jean le Fèvre, who used it in a poem he composed in 1376 as he was himself recovering from the plague.

- Like the other art forms we've discussed, this artistic theme probably existed before the arrival of the Black Death, but with the onslaught of plague, it became an increasingly popular subject for representation.

- In *danse macabre* paintings, drawings, and woodcuts, Death, represented as a skeleton, is usually shown engaging in a very enthusiastic dance, sometimes with other skeletons. Most often, the skeleton or skeletons are shown holding hands with a long line of living people, "dancing" them away to their deaths.

- The key point in all *danse macabre* representations is that every member of society is shown as participating. For example, you'll often see a clergyman holding hands with a farmer, who is holding the hand of a child, who might be holding the hand of king. Or sometimes the three of society are represented in descending order—kings and popes are first, then the lower ranks of society, all the way down to the lowliest peasants. The message is pretty clear: Death is the great equalizer.

- Many of the *danse macabre* works have been lost down through the ages, but we know they existed because people mentioned them. At the cemetery of Les Innocents in Paris, for example, there was a very influential depiction of the *danse macabre* in a mural on one of the walls of the cemetery, accompanied by Jean le Fevre's poem on the subject. Les Innocents no longer exists, so this mural is lost to time, but judging from personal accounts from the period, it seems to have made a huge impression on all those who saw it.

- The *danse macabre* was a popular subject not only in paintings and drawings but also in dramatic performances. In these allegorical dramas that were often part of some sort of religious service, the figure of death would usually ask characters representing all levels of society, one by one, to dance with him. While the characters could not refuse, they were portrayed as having one choice to make—salvation or damnation. The message here is clear: Repent now and clean up your life before death comes to take you!

- A variation on the theme of the dance of death was the triumph of death. In these representations, no one is dancing—rather, Death is depicted as a warrior who fights against the living.

- The great Petrarch, the first poet laureate since the days of the Roman Empire, had written a treatise in the 1340s on the triumph of fame. In 1348, with plague everywhere, he rewrote this work to be about the triumph of death, and it was his treatise in part that brought the theme to all the corners of the medieval world.

- In most depictions of the triumph of death, Death is a skeleton who triumphs over his prey by plunging a sword into them. A painting in Subiaco, Italy, depicts exactly this, and it's a terrifying image of a skeleton with a gruesome grimace and long flowing hair striking down an unsuspecting nobleman.

- The triumph of death theme in visual form was particularly popular in Italy. Not only is it the main subject of paintings in Subaico and Palermo, but there are many others, including one in the Camposanto Monumentale in Pisa.

- In the 1360s, a painter named Francesco Traini completed a series of frescoes for the Campo, which include such cheery subjects as the *Crucifixion*, the *Last Judgment*, the *Inferno*, and *Il Trionfo della Morte*—the triumph of death. There is some scholarly debate about the date of these paintings, with some experts suggesting that they were completed before 1348 and the onslaught of plague.

- If it was completed before 1348—and some still hold to the 1360 date— then at the very least, it was an image that must have seemed very apt to those who were living through the Black Death. It is a truly horrifying image, but one that we cannot fully appreciate today because the fresco was badly damaged during Allied raids on Italy during WWII.

- One might argue that the triumph of death motif reaches its apogee in the painting of the same name by Pieter Bruegel the Elder. His painting combines elements of the *danse macabre* tradition—which was called the *Totentanz* in Germany and *Dodendans* in the Netherlands—and the themes found in earlier triumph of death paintings.

- His painting is set in a landscape that includes a river, the sea, hills, a castle, and other geographical and architectural details. In other words, this background suggests the whole world. That world is bleak, full of smoke and fire, and looks like the aftermath of a great battle. The painting has a cast of thousands—pretty much every class, profession, rank, and occupation is represented here, and skeletons are carrying all of them off.

ARS MORIENDI

- These artistic representations were the outgrowth of an allegorical literary tradition—usually didactic poems—meant to remind people what death was. Just as the literary tradition evolved into a visual artistic tradition in the aftermath of the plague, so too did it evolve along another branch, into something called the *ars moriendi*, or "art of dying."

- This was a literary trend that became especially prominent in the 15th century, and it was based ultimately on two Latin texts from the period that offered Christians advice on how to live a good life so that when it came time to die, they might have the best chance possible of going to heaven. These works were incredibly popular and translated from Latin into almost every vernacular language on the European continent.

- The long version of the text contains six sections. Section one admonishes the reader not to be afraid of death. The second section identifies temptations that a person on the point of dying must beware of, including despair, pride, impatience, avarice, and lack of faith.

- The third section lays out seven questions that one should ask a dying person. The fourth is concerned with counseling people to try and imitate the example of Christ while still alive.

- The fifth section is concerned with practical matters of death and dying: Where should the family stand around the deathbed? What things should be said or not said? What sort of comforts should be offered? The text wraps up with a final section detailing the prayers that should be said on the occasion of a person's death.

- Many of these surviving texts are accompanied by woodcuts, some of which depict the personifications of the temptations, with the devil represented as encouraging these temptations.

- In a version of the text that dates from the Netherlands in the mid–15th century, these images of temptation are paired with others that illustrate how one should counter the devil's attempts to lure one into sin, and thus hell, on the eve of one's death.

- Perhaps the most famous of these woodcut images were done by the artist Hans Holbein the Younger. He made them to accompany a printed edition of the text that first appeared in 1524. In this version, the skeletons are not exactly dancing, but they do lead several victims from various classes away to their deaths.

QUESTIONS TO CONSIDER

1. Can you think of modern artistic responses to a crisis—war, plague, famine, etc.—that are comparable to those we see in the medieval world?

2. Which image or tradition seems most interesting or surprising to you?

SUGGESTED READING

Boeckl, *Images of Plague and Pestilence.*

Meiss, *Painting in Florence and Siena after the Black Death.*

LITERARY RESPONSES TO THE BLACK DEATH

I n this lecture, we're going to cover how some of the greatest literature the world has ever produced came into existence as a direct result of the plague. If ever there was a silver lining to be found, the fact that the Black Death gave writers like Giovanni Boccaccio and Geoffrey Chaucer the opportunity to create works of art that are still considered masterpieces today is it. But we'll start this lecture with a more predictable literary response to the plague: medical tracts.

MEDICINE

- In the midst of the first wave, those who practiced medicine were pressed into service to try and explain what was happening. The king of France commissioned the medical faculty of the University of Paris to write a *consilium*, or medical treatise, regarding the plague. This treatise spent a great deal of time explaining how the conjunction of Mars, Saturn, and Jupiter were to blame, as were the weather and the occurrence of several earthquakes.

- Diagnosis and treatment were based on Galenic medicine—named for the Greek physician Galen, who lived in the second century. Galen theorized that health of an individual dependent on the four humors—blood, phlegm, black bile, and yellow bile—being in balance or harmony. It was pretty much useless.

- While *consilia* had been a literary tradition before the arrival of the plague, between 1348 and 1350 there were medical professionals throughout the medieval world producing a veritable flood of them—around 900, according to the estimates of some scholars.

- While most are formal, technical documents, some are written as letters to the leaders of a particular community. For example, five physicians in Strasbourg composed theirs as a collaborative effort, addressed it to the leaders of that town, and entitled their work *The Treasure of Wisdom and Art*. Some treatises were actually written in verse.

PIERS PLOWMAN

- The Great Mortality had completely discombobulated the longstanding social order of the three estates—those who fight, those who pray, and those who work. A rising merchant class that didn't quite fit had been coming into their own just before the plague struck.

- The arrival of the Black Death accentuated and enhanced the way in which this group challenged the rigidity of the three estates model, because suddenly there were boundless economic opportunities for those who survived. The peasants were able to become clergy; the merchants were gaining increased wealth and status; and the nobles, cash-strapped and short of laborers to work their lands, started to do what had been unimaginable just a few years before—they started marrying members of the merchant class.

- The English writer William Langland explored the effect this had on society in his allegorical dream-vision poem known as *Piers Plowman*. In this poem, a man named Will has a series of dreams that offer instruction and commentary on how to live properly. Will's dream vision guide is a figure known as Piers the Plowman. This choice is interesting, because it's not a knight or bishop or other religious figure that guides Will on this quest, but a member of the lowest order of society.

- In the poem, Piers offers plenty of criticism of corrupt members of all classes. In particular, the Church receives a large share of criticism, and in one famous scene, Piers takes a pardon that has been issued by the Church and tears it in half in anger, an act that most have seen as a reaction against the buying and selling of forgiveness of sins by corrupt members of the clergy.

GIOVANNI BOCCACCIO

Giovanni Boccaccio

- The poem also offers a very conservative view of how society should be ordered: Society would be best served if people stayed in their estate and worked to be the best knight or bishop or plowman they could be. Even though this was Langland's intent, the poem later was used by the leaders of an uprising to promote their cause: The leaders of the English Uprising of 1381 saw in *Piers Plowman* a justification for the upward movement of the lower classes.

DECAMERON

- Of all the literature inspired by the plague, the most important is Giovanni Boccaccio's *Decameron*. The premise of the *Decameron* is that a group of noble youths have fled plague-ravaged Florence and headed to an estate in the country to wait until the Black Death has finished with the city.

- In order to pass the time, the young nobles take turns telling stories. There are 10 of them—seven young women and three young men—and each must tell a story every night for two weeks, with two nights off each week for the completion of chores and other necessary activities. Thus, at the end of 10 nights of storytelling, the group will have heard 100 stories—hence the title *Decameron*, which comes from the Greek words for "ten" and "day."

- This frame story of the nobles telling tales to pass the time is an ingenious way of grouping together stories from all different genres into one text, allowing Boccaccio to include stories that deal with holy saints, ribald and risque stories about adulterous husbands and wives, moral fables that impart a lesson, medieval romance stories about knights and chivalry, and everything in between.

- Boccaccio had completed the work by 1353, just as the first wave of the plague was dying down to smoldering embers in the medieval world. He chose to write the text not in Latin, as most scholars would have at the time, but in his native Florentine dialect of Italian, which made it accessible to a broader audience beyond the clergy.

- The stories themselves were borrowed from other sources—this was a standard practice for writers in the Middle Ages—but Boccaccio made them his own by recasting all the characters and events to reflect 14th-century Italian culture. Here and there he even put real historical figures into the stories. He also took basic plotlines and deliberately complexified them, making them much more interesting and nuanced in the process.

- The part of the *Decameron* that gets the most attention is Boccaccio's introduction, in which he details the horrors that the Black Death had wrought on the city of Florence. Boccaccio describes accurately the buboes that appeared on those afflicted with plague, the desertion of people by their family members once it became clear that they were infected with plague, the mass burials that took place at the height of the epidemic, and the terrifying rapidity with which the disease could spread from one person to another.

GEOFFREY CHAUCER

- Geoffrey Chaucer, the father of English poetry, was deeply influenced by Boccaccio. Indeed, his "The Knight's Tale" is a version of Boccaccio's *Teseida*, "The Reeve's Tale" is based on one of the stories told in the *Decameron*, and his masterpiece, *Troilus and Criseyde*, was based on Boccaccio's *Il Filostrato*.

- Chaucer's unfinished masterpiece, *The Canterbury Tales*, took the *Decameron* as its source for the idea of structuring a collection of tales. And just as Boccaccio was an innovator and reviser of existing narratives, so too did Chaucer rework the material and themes he found in Boccaccio to put his own definitive stamp on the texts he composed.

- Whereas Boccaccio's *Decameron* consists of tales told by a group of nobles, all of whom seem rather flat in terms of characterization and almost interchangeable, Chaucer's storytellers are representatives drawn primarily from the three orders of society, and they are all skillfully and cleverly individualized.

Geoffrey Chaucer

- He contrives a means to get members of all the orders of society together by coming up with the idea of a larger group of people traveling from London to Canterbury on a pilgrimage to the shrine of Thomas Becket. Along the way, these pilgrims partake in a storytelling contest to pass the time.

- While Chaucer's pilgrim group contains stock characters—a valiant knight; a noble squire, who is mostly interested in singing, dancing, and women; a corrupt friar; a dishonest miller; and more—he also includes several characters that don't quite fit into the three estates: the Wife of Bath, who is five times married and a member of the merchant class engaged in the cloth trade; a shipman; a doctor; a man of law; and several others.

- Chaucer began work on it in the late 1380s, after several outbreaks of plague had discombobulated the social order. By then, with the three estates model broken down and society remaking itself in a new image, *The Canterbury Tales* seemed a timely commentary on the current state of the world.

- One part, "The Pardoner's Tale," is set in a world where people are being struck down left and right by the Black Death. In that tale, three companions, upset about how many people Death has carried off, decide to go out and find Death and kill him. They ask an old man if he can show them where Death is, and he obliges.
  - When the companions arrive at the spot, however, they find not death but a pile of gold. Each of them tries to contrive a way to keep the gold for himself.
  - When one of them goes to town to fetch food and drink so that they can feed themselves while they watch over the gold that night, the two who remain behind plot to kill him.
  - Meanwhile, the third man poisons the wine he brings back with him. Upon his return, the two waiting with the gold kill him. After he's dead, they sit down and have a drink, and then die agonizing deaths. The three men, indeed, find Death.

CHAUCER'S FORMATION

- The plague sparked Chaucer's transformation into a literary master. In 1357, Chaucer was serving as a page in the household of Elizabeth de Burgh, countess of Ulster. Due to his presence in this household, Chaucer was close to the inner circle of the royal family. Young Chaucer seems to have acquitted himself well, and soon rose up the ranks as a civil servant.

- Then, in 1369, Blanche of Lancaster, wife of John of Gaunt, the son of Edward III and the richest man in England, died of plague. This is where Chaucer set off down the path of English poetry. In response to Blanche's death, he composed the dream vision poem known as *The Book of the Duchess.*

- At the center of the poem, the dreamer encounters a noble knight who is lamenting the loss of his lady. When pressed, the knight tells the dreamer that he was playing a game of chess with fortune, and fortune beat him and took his queen.

- Clearly, this is an allegorical chess game—but the dreamer takes the knight's story literally, telling him not to be so sad over losing a game. The knight then proceeds to tell the story of his sorrows—how he first fell in love with his lady (whom he calls "White," a play on the Duchess of Lancaster's name, "Blanche"), how it took a long time for White to reciprocate his love, but how once she did, their life together was perfect.

- Finally, he reveals that White is dead. With this last piece of information, the dreamer suddenly understands that this is not a chess game at all. The poem ends with the dreamer waking in his chamber, remembering his dream, and deciding that it should be set into verse.

- Some scholars think the poem was composed at Gaunt's request, others that Chaucer undertook the project on his own and presented it to the Duke of Lancaster as a commemoration of his wife. Whichever version is correct, the writing of this poem is what set Chaucer on a path that led away from civil service and diplomacy, and toward literary immortality.

QUESTIONS TO CONSIDER

1. Would you agree that this lecture and the previous one suggest that there is always some good to be found in any situation? Or would you say that, as stunning as these works of art are, the price that humanity paid was just too high?

2. Are there modern pieces of literature that you can think of that seem to be a response to a social tragedy or disaster? How do they differ from literature born out of the Black Death years?

SUGGESTED READING

Boccaccio, *Decameron.*

Howard, *Chaucer.*

THE ECONOMICS OF THE BLACK DEATH

T he epidemic that swept through the medieval world between 1347 and 1353 dramatically affected every aspect of life for every person who lived through the Great Mortality. Whether it was hit directly or not, every town, village, city, and nation changed in response to the plague. In this lecture, we're going to explore the economic impact of the Black Death on the medieval world. We'll stick to the broad economic trends that the Black Death both undermined and created.

LOSSES

- The most obvious and immediate effect of the first wave of the Black Death was the loss of laborers, both skilled and unskilled. Much in the way of technique and trade secrets was lost in the aftermath of the first pandemic. This meant that people suddenly had to forge new economic and trade relationships almost overnight.

- For example, if there were no blacksmiths in your town because all of them died, that didn't change the fact that you still need to have your horse shod. You might have to go to the next town over and use the services of that blacksmith, if he'd survived.

- Additionally, the coffers of most civic institutions were being drained by necessary expenditures, just as the tax base was shrinking. In Florence, for example, people coming from Pisa were forbidden from entering the city, but enforcing this rule required a heavily manned cordon at the various entrances to Florentine territory. Those people needed to be paid.

- Other necessary expenditures included buying up tracts of land and designating them as cemeteries in order to accommodate the huge number of burials that suddenly needed to take place. There were also huge numbers of widows and orphans who needed charitable assistance.

- The economic strain on civic entities wouldn't have been so bad, except for the fact that the tax base cities and nations depended on was suddenly cut in half. Sometimes the losses to the tax base were even greater.

- Numerous heads of households were suddenly gone—either as victims of the plague or because they had fled the city and headed to the countryside to wait out the worst of the epidemic. This in turn created many vacant houses.

- In the countryside, so many had died that livestock and farmland went untended. Cows, pigs, horses, and goats reportedly roamed freely, with no one to feed or milk them. In fact, there was such a surplus of livestock that we even have evidence of several lords of various manor estates in England turning down the payment of horse that should have been part of the heriot, or death tax.

MOVEMENT

- Peasants who had once resigned themselves to a lifetime of scratching out a subsistence living suddenly saw an opportunity for a better life— perhaps in the cities, which were in many cases almost empty. In many instances, newcomers placed yet an additional strain on the civic coffers.

- In a society that was structured hierarchically in terms of relationships of service, dependence, loyalty, and protection, new strategies needed to be developed to cope with the sudden appearance of groups of people who could move throughout the countryside wherever they liked. Again, this is a task that would require more civic officials to figure out and then execute, costing yet more tax money.

- But laborers in the countryside didn't only head to the cities. In many instances, they headed just down the road, to the next manor or landholder's property. Many landowners found themselves willing or needing to pay cash wages for able bodies who were willing to work.

- This was still not enough to prevent the prices of grain and produce from increasing sharply in the two decades after the first outbreak of the Black Death. Even though there was more than enough to go around, some people still suffered some serious privation in the immediate aftermath of the Great Mortality's arrival.

ABANDONMENT AND CONCENTRATION

- In some places where the plague hit especially hard, the citizens of a town that had been reduced to less than half its size and population might decide it would be better to pull up stakes and move to another community. Thus, many smaller towns and cities were abandoned altogether, and the population began to concentrate in clusters.

- This hadn't been possible in the early 1340s, because the population of Europe had gotten so large—doubling from 75 million in 1000 to about 150 million in 1300—that there had been a serious land crunch. Now, there was plenty of land to be had.

- Throughout the medieval world, but particularly in the Tuscan countryside, this trend was advanced by the practice of many urban merchants who saw a chance to become landowners. They bought up large parcels of land, joining together this piece and that piece for low prices. They then actively sought out laborers to work the land, establishing *mezzadria* (or formal sharecropping practices) that were quite favorable to the laborers.

- In the farms, cities, and trade centers, there occurred concentration and specialization. Before the plague each medieval community, even the smallest, was usually diverse enough to meet all its inhabitants' needs. Agriculture was the main profession of everyone, yes, but most communities had a blacksmith, a butcher, a brewer, a miller, and so on. In the aftermath of the Black Death, with half the population gone, people tended to concentrate in cities, and smaller communities joined forces.

- Medieval markets—sometimes called *fairs* when they were quite large— also became more specialized. Rather than a general market for goods, there might be a market for cloth and leather, a market for produce, a market for metalworkers and woodworkers, and so on.

WORKING WOMEN

- While women had always been contributors to the medieval economy in a limited capacity, many of them now stepped up and became full-fledged members of various occupations and trades. If your husband had been, for example, an apothecary, then as his wife, you'd probably assisted with making up the mixtures that were your stock-in-trade. If he died of the plague, then you most likely would just step up and take over so that you could keep feeding your family.

- One side effect was that women did not have as many children as they had in the past. In part, this was because they were often working at jobs that they would not usually have been. Additionally, the increase of disposable income meant a more upscale, comfortable lifestyle. Many women seem to have opted not to have children so that they could enjoy their money-enhanced quality of life.

- This, in turn, kept birth rates so low that the demographic rebound was not happening as quickly as people might have hoped. With there being another plague outbreak every decade or so for the next 200 years, the population would take centuries to recover.

WEALTH CONCENTRATION

- Generally speaking, a whole lot of wealth started to get concentrated with just a few people. If you were lucky enough to survive the first wave, you were probably the inheritor of all kinds of money and property from your various relatives who had passed away. The Church also received significant amounts from the deceased.

- Life changed dramatically for almost everyone, and it tended to change for the better. Serfs were able to become tenant farmers, or even enter professions that had previously been closed to them, like the order of the clergy.

- By the 14th century, most families throughout the medieval world were practicing primogeniture. They had figured out that if you divide property and wealth equally among heirs, you quickly dilute the inheritance. For instance, a large estate could break down into small, subsistence-level plots of land within a couple of generations.

- To counter that, the primogeniture system meant that the eldest son inherited pretty much everything. Second sons and daughters had to marry well or else join a religious order, and even doing that usually cost a substantial amount of money—a gift that the family made to the monastery or convent when they accepted the child into its ranks.

- But in the aftermath of the plague, the ranks of the clergy opened their doors to people farther down the social order, a fact that dramatically changed the nature and character of the medieval Church. The Church could do this, in part, because it was now less dependent upon the donations—or dowries—that such admittance usually brought with it, because the Church itself became a concentrated site of wealth in the face of so many deaths and bequests.

- It wasn't only the Church that found itself with so much surplus wealth, though. Plenty of individuals who had been living modest lives found themselves, all of a sudden, large landholders or possessors of other valuable property. With this excess wealth, they could do things like send their children to excellent schools to be educated.

- This was probably the case with Geoffrey Chaucer's family. The Chaucers were already rather-well-to-do members of the growing merchant class and had long been involved in the wine trade. Just by the sheer luck of surviving the Black Death, if you were a vintner or a cloth merchant, you might find yourself with a virtual monopoly in a particular market.

SOCIAL CLASSES

- The plague sped the rise of the already up-and-coming merchant class. This group was already somewhat complicating the ideal of the three estates model before the Black Death came on the scene.

- The orders of nobles, clergy, and everyone else had remained entrenched quite easily when the medieval world was a primarily agrarian society. But by the 14th century, with trade networks and a cash economy coming into its own, the merchants could only rather tentatively be contained within the "everyone else" category. With the arrival of the plague, they suddenly had more money than they knew what to do with.

- Soon, many merchants had acquired wealth on par with the nobles, who had lost substantial holdings and income because of the lack of laborers to work their land. Those laborers who remained could and did demand higher wages, and in many cases left the land on which they and their families had lived for years in search of better pay and opportunities for advancement elsewhere.

- Desperate to maintain their status and distinction from the rest of medieval society, many nobles got behind the passage of sumptuary laws, which restricted the kinds of clothes that could be worn by people of particular ranks. For example, in many places the law did not permit certain kinds of fur or silk trim for members below the ranks of the nobility.

- In the end, the social ideal of the three estates was undone by a phenomenon that could not have been imagined 50 years earlier. Cash-strapped nobles, desperate for income with which to pay for the laborers they needed to keep their estates running, started to marry members of the merchant class, who were themselves suddenly wealthy but also deeply desirous of climbing up the social ladder.

- A title was what well-to-do merchant families wanted more than anything. This narrative played out in Geoffrey Chaucer's own family—his granddaughter, Alice, became the duchess of Suffolk.

QUESTIONS TO CONSIDER

1. What seems the most predictable economic outcome of the Black Death? What result was most surprising to you?

2. What do you think European (and by extension, North American) society would look like today if the Black Death had never happened? Would a rigid socioeconomic structure like that of the medieval world still be in place, or do you think that eventually would have collapsed, even without the pandemic?

SUGGESTED READING

Hatcher, *Plague, Population, and the English Economy, 1348–1530.*

Livi-Bacci, *The Population of Europe.*

THE BLACK DEATH'S POLITICAL OUTCOMES

I n this lecture, we're going to look at how the political scene in several places throughout the medieval world was dramatically changed as a result the chaos that the Black Death had unleashed. We'll see that, in many instances, governments tried to maintain the status quo in a world that was nothing like the one out of which earlier social and political ideals—like the three estates model—had arisen. In the aftermath of the Great Pestilence, the world changed for the better for most people. Not surprisingly, when governments tried to force the genie of opportunity and social mobility back in the bottle, it did not go.

THREE TERMS

- The world's changes as a result of the Black Death occurred in three very distinct stages—the short term, the long term, and the extended term. In the short term, law and order and so many of the hallmarks of civilization fell by the wayside.

- In the long term, however, most political and governing bodies proved to be resilient and bounced back from the trauma of the plague pretty quickly.

- If we consider the extended term, we find that the world was utterly changed by the plague. While the long-standing governing structures were able to remain in place, they had to adapt to a new world in which the lower classes had more social and economic power and status than before.

AFTER THE BLACK DEATH: FLORENCE

- Once the first wave of the epidemic had passed, normalcy was restored in most places, but while the governing structures like councils and guilds were back in place, the composition of those bodies looked very different because of the impact. Two examples from Italy and England show how this happened.

- Florence was especially hard hit by plague in 1348, and then again in 1363 and 1370. While some semblance of civic order was maintained, taxes and fines had to be levied against those who fled the city and shirked their duties.

- One of Florence's most important exports was wool. Once the first wave of plague had passed, Florence was desperate to bring in revenue by increasing its production of wool back to pre-plague levels. In order to do this, it needed more laborers, and it found them out in the countryside.

- These laborers eventually came to be called the *gente nuova*—or "new people"—and even though they acquired some measure of wealth, they were not able to manage any sort of presence in local government because that was a position reserved for those of aristocratic status. Nonetheless, they were taxed and became disgruntled. The *gente nuova* found common cause with another disgruntled faction of the citizenry—the *arti minori*.

- The *arti minori*, or minor guilds, were those guilds that were considered second tier in the political system of Florence. They had long had a contentious relationship with the *arti maggiori*, seven powerful major guilds.

- There was also tension between the guilds and the ruling classes and a group known as the *popolo minuto*—literally, the "little people." In the ranks of the little people were all kinds of artisans whose work was essential to the cloth trade, but they did not have guild representation.

- In some cases, these groups overlapped—some *gente nuova* were also *popolo minuto*, and some were members of the *arti minori*. There was also a middle tier of guilds, the *arti medie*, whose interests could sometimes align with the *arti maggiori* and sometimes with the *arti minori*.

- On top of all this, those in power tried to re-impose a pre-plague governance system on those who were living and working in Florence, without really trying to adapt at all to this new reality. So, in 1378, the Ciompi revolt began. *Ciompi* is the word that designated the wool-carders of Florence, but many other groups were involved in the revolt.

- The revolt started with the Ciompi demanding better representation among the civic officials of Florence. The ruling oligarchy responded in a way that might have worked in a pre-plague world—they made it harder to get into a guild, and quadrupled the fee that people were required to pay for membership. In other words, instead of becoming more representative in response to these demands, they became more elitist.

- As a result, some limited violence broke out in late June, with members of the Ciompi and their affiliates attacking some government buildings and letting prisoners out of jail. In reaction to this, the ruling body of Florence, the Signoria, agreed to talks with the Ciompi.

- The government adopted some vague half measures. All this did was make the rebels even angrier. Many historians agree that if the Signoria had sincerely given just a little in the way of status and power to the lower classes, the whole Ciompi rebellion might have been avoided.

- On July 21, 1378, a full-blown rebellion broke out. Thousands of Ciompi and their associates forcibly ousted the members of the Signoria and placed one of their own in the powerful position of gonfaloniere of justice. They took the official executioner and hanged him by his feet in the Palazzo Vecchio.

- They demanded that the Signoria create three new official guilds and also decree that members of these guilds would hold public office. What they wanted, essentially, was representation for those in the *arti minori* and for the guildless *popolo minuto* to be given a guild with a voice in civic affairs.

- For three years, the government of the city-state of Florence was run by members of the Ciompi guild. But soon factionalism arose among members of the Ciompi, and in August 1378, fighting broke out among the Ciompi and other guild factions.

Palazzo Vecchio

- The civic leaders were replaced in one of the bloodiest days in Florence's history. But they were replaced by other members of the lower classes, and the city would continue to be ruled by them until 1382, when members of the aristocracy were able to rally together and oust the Ciompi and their allies from positions of civic leadership.

- Once the aristocratic patriciate was back in power, they sought both to shore up their position while also going ahead and enacting some of the reforms the Ciompi had wanted—in particular, a change in the tax system. In the extended term, Florence tried to return to what it had been like before the plague, but there was a new awareness of the power of the lower classes, and a greater concern with protecting the interests of the elite noble families.

AFTER THE BLACK DEATH: ENGLAND

- Almost immediately after the Black Death had swept through England, serfs who had been tied to manorial lands started pulling up stakes and looking for estates whose lords were willing to pay more for their labor. Many left agriculture altogether and headed into the cities in search of opportunities among the tradesmen and merchants there.

- In 1351, King Edward III and the British Parliament passed the Statute of Laborers. This law decreed that all wages should be frozen at pre-plague levels, and it stipulated that there would be no more roaming around the countryside in search of the best deal for one's labor, barring a lord's permission.

- This did not go over well. We know this from the ongoing passage of laws meant to keep laborers, and the lower classes in general, in their place. In 1361, laws were passed affirming the Statute of Laborers and adding penalties for violating it that included imprisonment and even branding.

- In practice, justices only punished members of the lower classes who broke the statute. Nobles who attempted to illegally outbid other nobles in order to secure workers generally got off scot-free. This meant that there was a huge incentive for peasants to violate the statute and go wherever the pay was greater.

- By one estimate, the purchasing power of the third estate—those who work—increased a dramatic 40 percent between 1340 and 1380. They could now not only buy goods and services previously unavailable to them, but they could also buy themselves and their children an education or secure for them apprenticeships in professions that had previously been closed to them.

- Legislation passed in 1363 limited what members of the lower class could wear or own; luxury goods and apparel were reserved for the upper class. The lower classes were starting to look and act more like the nobility, and the nobles did not want this to happen.

- The other major factor that contributed to political unrest at this point was England's war with France, probably better known as the Hundred Years' War. Because so much of the population had died off during the Black Death, there was a smaller taxable population, and this meant less money to support the war effort.

- In 1377, Parliament levied a poll tax, which demanded that every person over the age of 14 pay four pence toward the war effort. An already angry general population was ready to revolt.

- What happened in 1381 in London is sometimes called the Peasants' Revolt, but is also known as the Uprising of 1381. The latter name recognizes it wasn't just peasants and agricultural laborers who revolted: Plenty of the urban bourgeoisie and the very powerful London guilds participated as well. It came about because, once again, in the short term the world had changed dramatically.

- In the long term—the three decades or so after the plague—the political and economic infrastructures tried to reestablish themselves according to pre-plague principles, but that clearly wasn't going to work.

- When a London official traveled to Kent in 1381 to investigate nonpayment of the recently decreed poll tax, a large group of people, led by a Kentish man named Wat Tyler, rose up and not only revolted against authorities in Kent, but also marched on London. They eventually burned Savoy Palace and executed the archbishop of Canterbury with several other powerful government figures at the Tower of London.

- When the rebels and the king finally met to parley, the terms put forth by Wat Tyler included the abolishment of serfdom; demands that governance of small communities be overseen by those communities themselves, rather than by the crown; that certain hated government officials be handed over for execution; and that all the rebels be granted amnesty. Richard agreed to immediately have charters sent out officially abolishing serfdom, and it looked for a moment like the rebels had won the day.

- But they pushed too far. Instead of leaving the city and returning home, they made more demands a day later, and in that meeting Wat Tyler actually referred to the king as "brother" and said that it was OK with him if from now on he and Richard could consider themselves friends. No one is entirely clear as to what happened next, but some sort of scuffle broke out, and Wat Tyler was killed.

- Although the rebellion was over and Richard tried to retract most of the charters he had granted, those at the top of the political pyramid remained concerned about the threat of rebellion erupting from the lower classes. After 1381, there would be no more poll taxes to finance the war in France. With no money to support the war effort, England was forced to pull back from its continental campaigns for many years.

- Although it was still technically a legal option, serfdom went into decline from this point onward. Wages for laborers continued to increase, and there continued to be social mobility of a sort that had never existed previously.

- Those who were in power had learned that they were now truly answerable to every level of society. It was this shift that paved the way for the Renaissance that was coming in the 16th century. In the extended term, institutions and organizations remained, but they were different in their powers and their interests.

QUESTIONS TO CONSIDER

1. Which social and political groups suffered the most because of the Black Death? Which ones benefited the most?

2. Do you think the Black Death contributed significantly to a movement toward more democratic forms of government, or is that an evolution that probably would have happened whether or not the plague ravaged the medieval world?

SUGGESTED READING

Palmer, *English Law in the Age of the Black Death, 1348–1381.*

Ziegler, *The Black Death.*

COMMUNITIES THAT SURVIVED THE FIRST WAVE

The Black Death of 1347–1353 killed off some 50 percent of Europe's population, with another significant segment of people contracting the disease but surviving it. It seems it would be safe to say that everyone in the medieval world was affected in that first wave of death. But were they? In fact, there were a few communities—and some entire nations—that were spared during the initial mid–14th century outbreak. How on earth did they manage this? In this lecture, we're going to look at several of these communities and see how swift civic action, luck, and sometimes a combination of the two played a part in sparing these fortunate few.

AVOIDING THE PLAGUE

- In a few cases, avoidance was a matter of simple geography. The Basque region, for example, is in the mountains between France and Spain, and part of its border is the ocean. It came through the first wave in decent shape because of geographical and cultural isolation.

- The country of Iceland enjoyed a degree of natural protection simply by virtue of the fact that it was an island. Timing factored in as well: In August 1349, an Icelandic trading ship that had traveled to Norway was preparing to return to Reykjavik from Bergen with new goods on board. Just before the ship was scheduled to set sail, a plague epidemic was recognized as having broken out on board, and the voyage was canceled. This event both saved the Icelandic population and made them extremely cautious about trading with countries and communities where there was even a rumor of plague.

- This meant that Iceland managed to avoid plague until there was finally an outbreak in 1402. As with the initial outbreaks in the medieval world 50 years earlier, mortality rates were estimated at around 50 percent. After

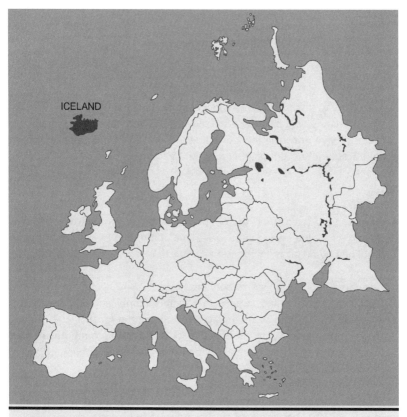

Iceland's relative isolation, along with some luck, helped it avoid plague for some time.

this experience, Iceland managed to avoid plague until they were hit with a second outbreak in 1494.

- The limited number of outbreaks in Iceland and the long periods between them is actually crucial to the fact of Iceland's very existence today. By some estimates, Iceland's medieval population had peaked at around 60,000 people in the year 1400—relatively small, especially considering the plague would eliminate 50 percent of those people. Frequent outbreaks would have been absolutely devastating.

- Another Scandinavian country that seems to have largely escaped the Black Death was Finland. Although this nation is connected to Sweden and Norway, it was a fairly isolated entity in the mid-14th century—almost like an island—and its population density was very low. These two factors seem to have done the most to allow Finland, like Iceland, to avoid any significant outbreak of plague until the 15th century.

POLAND

- Another very interesting case of supposed plague avoidance is medieval Poland. For a long time, there was a line of argument in historical circles that Poland had been only minimally affected.

- The most likely primary reason for Poland *appearing* to have escaped the Black Death by and large is that there's simply not very much data available for the time and the place. And the reason for this, according to the great plague historian Ole Benedictow, is that under communism, there was an active effort to suppress evidence of the socioeconomic impact of the Black Death.

- Since the communist belief system is predicated in large measure on the ideal of the working class rising to power under its own power, the fact that an external force like the plague contributed to making this possible throughout the medieval world was not something that fit into the narrative of how communism had come to be. There were plenty of people who had a vested interest in either not telling this story or actually actively suppressing it.

- In 1348, Poland was a very small, landlocked kingdom bordered by Prussia, Moldova, the German states, and what we consider today part of the Ukraine. Where once there seemed to be consensus that Poland had managed to escape the worst of the Black Death, in fact, it experienced it on a level similar to what was occurring throughout the rest of the medieval world.

- This makes sense, because unlike Finland or Iceland, where plague had only one viable route in and where this route was blocked or limited, the Black Death was coming at Poland from all sides—from the north, via Gdansk, which we know was hit in 1349; from the west, via the city of Frankfurt, a Polish trading partner that was overrun with plague in 1351; and from the south, via the river Vistula.

- Research into wages in the Middle Ages suggests that a demographic catastrophe did hit the region. For example, in Krakow in the 1350s, we see wages for laborers increase dramatically—just as they did in England, France, and most of Germany at the same time. All of those countries saw wages rise because there was a desperate need for bodies to work at a variety of jobs and professions.

- It's interesting to note that grain prices also fell at the same time. Benedictow argues that this is because, in the face of massive depopulation, agricultural lands that were poor producers of grain had been abandoned now that there were better, more productive fields for the taking.

- Some scholars have argued that while medieval Poland was affected, it managed to come out of the first wave of the epidemic with fewer casualties—instead of 50 percent, many think that the death rate was closer to 30 or 25 percent. That's still a huge number, but the lower death rates in Poland, if in fact they were lower, may be in part due to Poland's geography. It was one of the most densely forested portions of the medieval world, and there were long distances between villages, which meant it was difficult for plague to travel.

- Another argument: There were fewer black rats in Poland and the nearby Kingdom of Bohemia (which included much of the modern-day Czech Republic). Therefore, the black rat flea, the main host and transmitter of *Yersinia pestis*, was less likely to be found in these places. One reason, some scholars posit, is that there was less of the kind of food in these places that black rats like to scavenge.

MILAN'S ESCAPE

- One of the most surprising examples of a city that escaped infection is Milan. In 1348, this was one of the great cities among the Italian city-states. Like Florence, Rome, Genoa, and Pisa, Milan was an important center of government and trade. But while most of these other cities were either ports or had longstanding trade networks that made use of nearby port cities, Milan was a center primarily for overland trade.

- The progress of the plague overland was slower than the infection that moved in so rapidly from major port cities. But this fact alone is not what allowed Milan to make it to 1353 virtually unscathed by plague. The key difference here is in how Milan was governed.

- In contrast to places like Florence, Pisa, and Genoa, the ruler of Milan was an individual—not an oligarchy—and he was an absolute despot. He was a member of the powerful Visconti family. He could rely on his many relatives—who were also in positions of political and economic power in Milan—to back him up whenever he made a decision.

- In 1348, the Visconti ruler was Luchino. When he first learned of the outbreak of plague, he enacted extreme preventive measures. First, he significantly increased the guard presence at the gates of the city, and almost all movement of travelers into the city was halted.

- Still, despite this, plague did manage to make its way into Milan. When word came that there were three families in the city who had members who appeared to be suffering from plague, Luchino's successor, Bernabo Visconti, moved to have the houses in questions walled up from the outside, entombing not only the infected people, but their uninfected family members as well.

- Our scientific and medical understanding of exactly what happened in the mid-14th century is still evolving, and it's possible that certain diseases may confer some level of immunity to plague. One candidate in the list of immunity-conferring diseases is typhus.

- In early 1348, there was a typhus outbreak in Milan, and some experts theorize that this may have essentially inoculated much of the population against the plague, which appeared soon after. Whatever the reason, Milan's death rate was a very modest 15 percent—an unbelievable achievement when compared to the rest of the medieval world.

NUREMBERG

- Even more impressive was the situation in Nuremberg. This city was a major hub in terms of trade through and across the Alps, so it seems logical that it would have been severely affected once plague broke out. But according to some measures, Nuremberg had a mortality rate of only about 10 percent. Nuremberg may have been saved by the character of the city as a whole.

- At the time, Nuremberg was unique among Western European medieval cities for its high standards of public health. Unlike many European cities, in Nuremberg the streets were not only almost entirely paved, they were also regularly cleaned. Whereas plenty of other cities had open sewers into which people would dump trash or empty their chamber pots, in Nuremberg, by law all garbage had to be bagged up and carted away.

- In most towns and villages in the medieval world, it would have been a common sight to see pigs wandering about. This was because it was easier to simply let your pig run loose for most of the year, foraging for their meals, than it was to keep the animal enclosed and have to procure sustenance for it. In Nuremberg, pigs were not allowed to roam the streets.

- This, in combination with the edicts concerning trash, meant that the city itself was unusually clean. Cleanliness and good sanitation translates to fewer rats, which meant fewer fleas, which meant fewer occasions for plague to be transmitted to a human host.

- If the city employed high standards of sanitation and hygiene, then so did its citizens. In Nuremberg, there were 14 public bathhouses, and as far as we can tell, they were strictly regulated. In many other places, certain bathhouses were really brothels in disguise. Not in Nuremberg. In that city, regular inspections took place to make sure that everything was legitimate and that the facilities were kept clean.

- A city like this was quick to dispose of its dead as hygienically as possible. While in many other places the clothes in which someone had died might actually be taken off the corpse and given away or sold, in Nuremberg the clothing of the dead, plus all their bedding, was destroyed.

- Rooms in which people had died were required to be fumigated—meaning that some kind of strong-smelling herb, like sage, or some kind of incense would be lit in the room. The smoke would clear any foul odors from the air and also probably drive away rats and their fleas.

QUESTIONS TO CONSIDER

1. What do you think the single most important factor was in the survival of these communities when so many others succumbed to the plague?

2. Which of the strategies deployed by the communities of Milan, Nuremberg, etc. would be effective in the face of a modern pandemic?

SUGGESTED READING

Biow, "The Politics of Cleanliness in Northern Renaissance Italy."

Cantor, *In the Wake of the Plague.*

LATER PLAGUE OUTBREAKS: 1353–1666

T he first wave of the Black Death challenged the social, political, religious, and economic structures that had long been in place. Indeed, in some cases, the Great Mortality seemed likely to completely overthrow them. In 1353, when the first wave seemed to have burned itself out, we can imagine that people took a deep breath, looked around, and started to hope that life would get back to normal. They might have succeeded in restoring the medieval world to some semblance of what it had been in 1340, except that the plague began to recur with some regularity just about every 10 years or so.

PLAGUE RECURRENCES

1360–63	Next significant outbreak following the first wave	1544	
1374		1563	
1400		1573	
1438		1596	
1456		1602	A decade of plague begins
1464		1623	Almost two decades of plague begin
1481	Plague returns and stays for almost five years	1644	Another decade-long outbreak begins
1500		1664–67	The last major outbreak occurs
1518	Plague returns and stays for almost 15 years		

POPULATION IMPACTS

- These recurrences meant that demographically, the population of most of the medieval world was kept from recovering to pre-plague levels until as late as the 17th century. This definitely was the case with the plague outbreak of 1360–63, which targeted mostly the young: those who had been born after the first wave ended in 1353.

- In England, it seems that it was particularly males who were carried off in 1360–1361. Several chronicles make a point of mentioning this, including the *Chronicle of Louth Park Abbey*, which records the following entry: "In AD 1361 there was a mortality of men, especially of adolescents and boys, and as a result it was commonly called the pestilence of boys."

PREVIOUSLY SPARED COMMUNITIES

- Places like Iceland, Finland, Milan, and Nuremberg came through the first wave virtually unscathed. They were not so lucky with this next outbreak. Milan, which had come through the first wave with a mortality rate of just around 15 percent, was particularly devastated in 1361. Milan's luck seemed to have run out after its miraculous escape from the first wave, and for the next two centuries it was repeatedly hit by new outbreaks.

- Nuremberg, too, was unable to maintain its relative immunity. With a mortality rate of 10 percent, it had one of the best survival rates in the medieval world. But eventually it, too, was ravaged by plague—in 1405, 1435, 1437, and on several more occasions until 1534. But it had managed to avoid the most devastating wave of plague, and this fact alone meant that Nuremberg was poised to become the center of the German Renaissance in the 15th and 16th centuries.

- Iceland managed to avoid the plague for almost 50 years after the first outbreak. But eventually their luck would run out: When the plague struck that island nation in 1402, it carried off half the population. Many scholars see the years 1400–1800 as marked by a decline in Icelandic culture—a decline that began when the Black Death finally penetrated the natural defenses that the ocean had provided for half a century.

PESTHOUSES

- Most communities realized that the plague was going to come back with some regularity, and as such, it was necessary that there be some strategies in place to combat it. Italian cities like Florence took steps to create a "board of health" in the aftermath of the first outbreak. Soon, other cities instituted similar policies.

- One new creation that came into existence was the pesthouse, or *lazaretto*. Sometimes called *lazar houses*—after the biblical figure of Lazarus, whom Jesus raised from the dead—these were places where those sick with plague were sent to either die or recover.

- The Italian city-state of Venice was one of the first to institute this practice. They made use of the natural defenses of islands. It was in the Venetian territory of Dubrovnik, in what is now Croatia, that scholars think the first pesthouse was established. This was on the island of Mljet in 1377. In Venice itself, the city leaders had a plague hospital constructed in 1403.

- It is from the city-state of Venice that we get the first systematic use of the idea and word *quarantine*. The term comes from the Italian phrase *quaranta giorni*, or "forty days," which was the length of time Venice required ships and people to wait on a nearby island before they were permitted to enter the port city of Dubrovnik.

- Marseille, another one of the earliest hit cities during the first wave, instituted similar policies, building a facility specifically dedicated to the care of plague patients in 1383. Soon, pesthouses were being constructed or designated throughout the medieval world, in Milan, Florence, Barcelona, the German cities of Ulm and Uberlingen, and many more.

- Conditions in the pesthouses ranged from OK to horrific, depending on how bad the outbreak was. There was also the additional bureaucratic burden of staffing and supplying these pesthouses, and this meant a significant outlay on the part of local governments. The people who worked there were very likely to contract the disease themselves, so replacing them was another added burden that civic organizations had to constantly worry about.

- These establishments were regularly overcrowded: Data from Florence's lazaretto of San Miniato in 1630 show that there were 82 beds assigned to 412 female patients and 93 beds for 312 male patients.

- Pesthouses were universally hated by those who were removed to that location or had to watch loved ones carted off, most likely to die. We have evidence from many cities that mobs sometimes tried to burn down pesthouses.

- Because no one wants to send their loved one to a hellhole to die, plenty of families would try to hide the fact that one of their members was sick, and if they could afford it, smuggle them out of the city and away from the surveillance of authorities. In response, civic authorities levied fines, imposed prison sentences, or even executed people who tried to prevent themselves or family members from being sent away to the lazaretto. In some cases, people tried to escape or break out.

EYAM

- In one famous case from England, an entire village opted to quarantine itself. The Pulitzer Prize–winning novelist Geraldine Brooks tells the story of this village in her brilliant novel, *Year of Wonders*. In the year 1665, the village of Eyam in Derbyshire was infected with the plague.

- None of the villages around it were affected, which created a conundrum: how to contain the infection while still getting the food and supplies the community needed to survive. Under the guidance of the town's religious leaders, a series of rules went into effect in early 1666. These included the suspension of church services indoors, so as to avoid mingling of infected and uninfected persons; the edict that all families were to bury their own dead, whenever possible; and that no one would go down out of the village into neighboring towns.

- Through what one imagines was a shouted conversation with the leaders of the nearby communities, the people pledged to keep themselves quarantined in Eyam as long as the neighboring communities would drop off food and supplies at a designated spot.

- Nearby town officials agreed to this, and for 14 months, no one entered or left Eyam. While the disease didn't spread beyond the borders of the town, it did kill at least half of the population. Our best guess is that at least 260 people died out of an initial population of 350. Some say the numbers were more like 800 villagers in the beginning, with around 400 surviving. Whatever the specific numbers, the survival rates were bad.

LONDON

- The plague that came to Eyam was a side effect of the epidemic raging in London at the time. This outbreak was the last one of any real consequence in England. Although subsequent outbreaks after 1352 had tended to be much less virulent in nature, the Black Death in Britain went out with a bang rather than a whimper. The outbreak that ravaged London in 1665–1666 was appropriately known as the Great Plague of London, and it left an indelible stamp on the consciousness not just of England, but of the whole Western world.

- In 1664, British officials got troublesome reports of outbreaks of plague on the continent. They immediately tried to implement quarantine measures, but by the summer of 1665, the plague was rampant in London. The great diarist Samuel Pepys made a note of it in his journal, commenting on the number of houses that were being shut up and shut off so as to contain the plague.

- Those who could fled the city, including the royal family, who decamped for Salisbury. Daniel Defoe described the scene, stating: "Nothing was to be seen but wagons and carts, with goods, women, servants, children, etc.; coaches filled with people of the better sort, and horsemen attending them, and all hurrying away ...."

- In July, plague deaths increased every week at an exponential rate. Bodies were hastily buried in mass graves known as plague pits. According to one account, cartloads of dead were brought to one end of a plague pit and dumped in; at the other end, workers were digging furiously to enlarge the mass grave, but could barely keep up. The plague pit outside the district of Aldgate is estimated to have contained over 1,000 corpses.

- By September, one count has 7,000 people a week dying. That number is likely to be an underestimate, because when an epidemic of such virulence hits, whole families or neighborhoods are wiped out, and no one is left to record the numbers of the dead. Many records that *did* exist were destroyed in the Great Fire of London, which occurred in 1666.

- The Great Fire may be, in the end, what brought the epidemic to its end. Surely, plenty of rats and fleas perished, and when this most important link of the plague "food chain" was removed, the plague very likely lost almost all of its potency. In any event, while the plague was over, there were new infections that took its place, like smallpox.

- The Black Death didn't return to the world in any substantial form from the end of the 17th century to the end of the 19th. That's when the third plague pandemic arose in India and China. It was this outbreak that gave scientists their first lead as they tried to conclusively identify what it was that had killed off half the population of the medieval world in the mid–14th century.

- The bubonic plague has not disappeared entirely from the world—it's still found in parts of Asia and in the American Southwest, especially among rodent populations. In the 21st century in the U.S., there are usually between and 2 and 20 cases a year. If these are diagnosed early enough, they can usually be treated successfully with antibiotics, but in 2015 there were four deaths from plague—probably because it is one of the last things a medical professional is going to consider when presented with a patient who has symptoms that in many regards resemble the flu.

QUESTIONS TO CONSIDER

1. What had people learned from earlier epidemics and pandemics that helped them to weather later outbreaks of disease as the Middle Ages transformed into the Early Modern world—or had they learned anything?

2. Where do you think the greatest impact of the repeated recurrence of plague was felt—in the political, economic, or psychological realms?

SUGGESTED READING

Aberth, *From the Brink of Apocalypse.*

Cantor, *In the Wake of the Plague.*

How the Black Death Transformed the World

M any think the plague is gone, and that it no longer presents any sort of real threat to the modern world. Though that is mostly the case, the plague is far from eradicated or unimportant. In fact, one might argue that understanding the Black Death is more essential than ever in the 21st century. While it's certainly important to recognize how the Black Death changed the medieval world, this final lecture of the course will take a broader view and argue that one thing we can learn from that epidemic is how disease in general—and virulent pandemics like the plague in particular—have shaped human societies and individual behavior for all of recorded history and beyond.

REAPPEARANCE AND OTHER DISEASES

- The Black Death must have seemed a particularly horrible kind of plague, because it would periodically appear and disappear over the span of about three centuries. No one could know when an outbreak was really and truly over, and we can imagine that after 300 or so years of this, no one dared to get their hopes up that this outbreak might be the last. So when the last real outbreak of plague ended (for example, in London in 1666) there were no celebrations or sighs of relief—just more waiting for what might be coming next.

- If plague was largely done with the world, there were plenty more diseases to fill that vacuum. Although cases of smallpox have been recorded as far back as 1000 B.C., this disease didn't make a serious incursion into the Western European world until the 16th century. At this time, plague still recurred periodically, but its virulence was very much diminished. It was also in the 16th century that another disease, syphilis, appeared on the European scene. After that, there was cholera to contend with.

- At the end of the 19th century, plague reappeared for the first time with any significant impact in India and China. Intense study of this so-called Third Pandemic of plague is what helped scientists determine that this pandemic was caused by the same agent that was behind the Black Death and the Plague of Justinian.

- Then the influenza outbreak of 1918 came on the scene. It's estimated that 3–5 percent of the planet's population was wiped out before the pandemic finally came to an end. While there have been later outbreaks of influenza, many of them serious, none has quite reached the level of the 1918 pandemic—but such an outbreak could come some day.

- For each of these other later outbreaks of disease, the Black Death often functioned as a touchstone, as a comparison or filter or mechanism that would allow people the means to process current epidemics and figure out how to function and respond.

THE 21ST CENTURY

- At the end of the 20th century, the Black Death was pressed into service quite frequently to give people language to talk about the HIV/AIDS epidemic. In scholarship by medieval literary and scholars from the 1980s and 1990s in particular, the Black Death and HIV/AIDS are discussed alongside each other with astonishing frequency, with each being used to comment on the other.

- In the 21st century, with HIV/AIDS becoming a condition that was more and more treatable, pandemic interest and discussion turned elsewhere. Especially in 2014 and 2015, discussion shifted toward the viral hemorrhagic fever Ebola.

- When Ebola was first discovered and named, it was estimated to have mortality rates of around 90 percent. The virus gained much attention during a 2014 outbreak in West Africa. When medical staff treating a patient in the United States were infected, panic increased.

- The good news is that with intense treatment and extreme quarantine and isolation measures, the Ebola mortality rate dropped to something like 40 percent during the last part of the 2014 outbreak. The bad news, of course, is that the mortality rate is still around 40 percent, and the possibility of another outbreak remains.

PLAGUE TODAY

- While plague can now be treated with antibiotics and is not widespread, it still exists. 2015 saw more deaths from plague than 2014 and 2013 combined for the simple reason that no one recognized what it was in time. Granted, these deaths are still in the single digits, but it's a reminder that this ancient enemy is still around.

- While we have effective treatments, medical science has been sounding the alarm for some time now concerning what we have in place. Antibiotics are losing their ability to fight certain diseases, especially those caused by so-called superbugs, and while the pharmaceutical industry has ramped up its efforts to find new therapies and medications, progress on that front is not as fast as we might hope.

- Additionally, there's always the possibility of bacterial mutation. In fact, the Black Death may still be around in part because, after its initial virulent outbreak, it mutated to become less deadly. After all, a pathogen that kills off most of the hosts it needs to survive is also threatening its own existence. While *Yersinia pestis* today is arguably less lethal than it was in the 14th century, another mutation and transformation is always possible, and that mutation could go the other direction.

- Adding to this concern is the simple fact that the world is much more interconnected today than it was in 1348: International flights could be an extremely fast way for the plague to spread. One example is Thomas Eric Duncan, who traveled from Liberia to Dallas, Texas. While there, he was diagnosed with an eventually fatal case of Ebola, and two nurses who treated him at the hospital where he was admitted contracted the disease as well.

SURAT, INDIA

- Surprisingly to many, the Third Pandemic of the plague has never officially been declared over. Moreover, there was a 1994 plague epidemic in Surat, India, which eerily recalls many aspects of the Second Pandemic from the mid-14th century.

- For starters, there was the event that triggered the plague: an earthquake, just like so many of those medieval plague accounts described. An earthquake near the village of Mamla seems to have displaced large colonies of rats from their native territories. As they moved into areas with high concentrations of people, the plague made a jump to the human population.

- It wasn't caught quickly, because India, like many other countries, had stopped paying attention to or worrying about plague. Once the infection was established, it followed the movements of people—in this case, migrant workers who were heading into the city of Surat, which had a population of one and a half million.

- Another reason the plague could get a strong foothold: The form that swept through Surat was pneumonic, which in its earliest stages looks a whole lot like the flu. It's only when a lot of people suddenly start coughing up blood that someone might figure out that this is not simple influenza.

- The first infections raged through the slums of the city, where quarters were close, good health care nonexistent, and governmental oversight severely lacking. The plague grew to a tipping point where it could not be effectively contained anymore. It's estimated that 78 percent of confirmed cases of plague were in the slums of Surat.

- The rest of the story follows much of the template for plague reaction that we saw in the medieval world. Once health care officials did figure out what was going on and tried to react, they found they were woefully underprepared. There was a shortage of antibiotics. Medical professionals in the hardest hit areas abandoned their posts.

- In the medieval world, people moved around a lot when they just should have stayed put. In Surat, when the word got out (aided by heavy media coverage), people started fleeing the city in droves. They got onto tightly packed trains and headed to Delhi and Calcutta, bringing the disease with them.

- In a dishearteningly familiar occurrence, members of Surat's Muslim community were accused of spreading the plague directly in an act of bioterrorism by poisoning Surat's water system.

- But here's a major difference: Out of all those millions of people who panicked when they should have stayed calm, who moved when they should have stayed put, it's estimated that there were only about 5,000 or so cases of actual plague and only 53 deaths. That at least is a more heartening picture than what we get from studying the Second Pandemic in the 14th century.

- On the disheartening side: Shortly after the outbreak in Surat, plague was discovered on Madagascar. Alarmingly, one of the strains of *Yersinia pestis* found there is resistant to all known antibiotics used to treat plague. When *Yersinia pestis* comes in contact with other bacteria, it borrows material from them and rewrites its own genetic code. This process is called *lateral gene transfer*, and scientists have figured out that *Yersinia pestis* has recently borrowed from *E. coli* and salmonella. The lesson here is a chilling one, and it's one we would all do well to heed.

HUMAN RESILIENCE

- The best and most encouraging lesson we can take away from a study of the Black Death is that human beings are resilient. While accounts describe bodies lying in the streets and people fleeing friends and family to escape from the plague, they also tell of ordinary people stepping up and going to extraordinary extremes to offer help and comfort:
  - Parish priests who performed their duties humbly, many dying as a result.

- ▶ Figures like Saint Roch and Saint Carlo Borromeo, whose beatification can be traced directly to the fact that they risked their own lives to help others.
- ▶ The numerous leaders in government who tried to maintain normalcy and carry on with business as usual while coming up with plans to fight the plague.
- ▶ People who buried children and husbands and wives and then, somehow, managed to keep going.
- ▶ Artists and writers who looked at the horrors around them and produced something that was inspired and inspiring—that offered both commentary and comfort to a population who were trying to make sense of what was happening.

- Without the Black Death, we might not have the great works of the Italian writer Boccaccio, and without Boccaccio, there might have not have been Chaucer's *Canterbury Tales*.

- For that matter, without the Black Death, John of Gaunt's wife might not have died, and Chaucer might not have been inspired to write *The Book of the Duchess*, and John of Gaunt might not have decided to become a supporter and patron of Chaucer's creative work.

- Society as we know it might look a whole lot different, as class boundaries would surely have remained entrenched for much longer, and the Church would not have had to confront a crisis that undermined so much of its power.

- In the end, the important lessons of the Black Death and other plagues are about the people and communities who survived these illnesses. The losses were huge, but by and large, civilization remained. It had changed, but in our world today, which arose out of the medieval world, we are more like the people of the Middle Ages than we are different. This bodes well for the future of humanity, no matter what should come our way.

QUESTIONS TO CONSIDER

1. What similarities do you see in people's reactions to modern epidemics—like HIV/AIDS, Ebola, SARS, MERS, and Zika—and those of medieval people to the Black Death? Is there anything profoundly different in terms of individual and social/communal reactions?

2. Can humanity ever be truly prepared to contain and control an epidemic, especially in a modern, globalized world?

SUGGESTED READING

McNeill, *Plagues and Peoples.*

Wills, *Plagues.*

Bibliography

Aberth, John. *The Black Death: The Great Mortality of 1348–1350: A Brief History with Documents*. Boston and New York: Bedford St. Martin's, 2005. While not as comprehensive as Rosemary Horrox's collection of primary texts, still a fascinating collection of contemporary records with notes and an overview of the Black Death's effects.

Aberth, John. *From the Brink of Apocalypse: Confronting Famine, War, Plague, and Death in the Later Middle Ages*. 2nd ed. London and New York: Routledge, 2010. Focused primarily on England, this fascinating text examines how that society coped with a series of disasters—plagues, wars, famine, and other diseases—in the 15th century. Remarkable for the depictions of resiliency and fortitude among the population.

Bailey, Mark and Stephen Rigby, eds. *Town and Countryside in the Age of the Black Death: Essays in Honour of John Hatcher*. Turnhout, Belgium: Brepols, 2012. A collection of several articles by top scholars in the field. Divided into broad sections that include "The Medieval Demographic System," "Landlords and Peasants," and "Trade and Industry."

Benedictow, Ole J. *The Black Death 1346–1353: The Complete History*. Woodbridge: The Boydell Press, 2004. The definitive book on the subject by one of the leading plague scholars of the modern period. Can be a bit dry at times, but scrupulously precise, with a helpful and very clear map of plague progression between the years 1346–1353. Arguably, the book with which to start and end any discussion of the plague.

———. *The Black Death and Later Plague Epidemics in the Nordic Countries: Perspectives and Discoveries*. Berlin: de Gruyter, 2015. The latest scholarly work from one of the top plague scholars working today; fills in important gaps in our knowledge about how the plague affected Scandinavia.

Boeckl, Christine. *Images of Plague and Pestilence: Iconography and Iconology*. Kirksville, MO: Truman State University Press, 2000. Nicely illustrated volume that explores artistic responses to plague from the 14th century through to the 17th.

Brewer, Derek. *The World of Chaucer*. Cambridge: D.S. Brewer, 2000. A richly illustrated and highly informative survey of the life, times, and literary output of the father of English poetry.

Byrne, Joseph P. *The Black Death*. Westport, CT: Greenwood Press, 2004. Incredibly thorough study of the 14th century pandemic with chapters organized thematically with some very useful, detailed case studies. After Benedictow, Byrne looks to be the most important plague scholar of the 21st century.

———. *Daily Life During the Black Death*. Westport, CT: Greenwood Press, 2006. An attempt to bring the medieval world in its various aspects to life during the several decades of the medieval Black Death. Includes chapters like "At the Doctor's Office," "At Home With the Plague," "At the Bookseller's and the Theater." Also includes excerpts from primary documents.

———. *Encyclopedia of the Black Death*. (Santa Barbara: ABC-CLIO, 2012). Just as the title suggests—encyclopedic and wide-ranging, with entries on every subject conceivably linked to the Black Death. Invaluable.

Cohn, Samuel K. *The Cult of Remembrance and the Black Death*. Baltimore: Johns Hopkins University Press, 1992. This study focuses on Italy, paying particular attention to wills in later outbreaks of plague after the initial appearance of the disease on the Italian peninsula in 1347–8. Cohn's central argument is that the plague diminished religious piety but also made art and family relationships even more important than they had been previously.

Dohar, William J. *The Black Death and Pastoral Leadership: The Diocese of Hereford in the Fourteenth Century*. Philadelphia: University of Pennsylvania Press, 1995. Zeroes in on one particular monastic community to explore the ramifications of plague—both in its initial outbreak and subsequent ones.

Argues that after the initial chaos, the Hereford leadership found ways to manage the effects of plague.

Gies, Frances and Joseph Gies. *Daily Life in Medieval Times*. Grange Books, 2005. A compendium that includes the Gies' three classic works—*Life in a Medieval Village, Life in a Medieval Town, Life in a Medieval City*. Although not as scholarly rigorous as it might be, it remains a good basic introduction to the period, especially for YA readers. Plenty of photos, maps, and illustrations.

Gottfried, Robert S. *The Black Death: Natural and Human Disaster in Medieval Europe*. New York and London: Macmillan Publishing, 1983. Examines the Black Death from the angle of an ecological/environmental disaster. Takes care to pay attention to the demographic situation that set up a Malthusian crisis, which the plague took ample advantage of.

Green, Monica, ed. *Pandemic Disease in the Medieval World: Rethinking the Black Death*. Kalamazoo and Bradford: Arc Medieval Press, 2015. Collection of articles by the top scholars of today working on various aspects of the Black Death. Includes chapters on the impact of plague on Jewish communities, bioarchaeological analyses, the persistence of plague beyond the first outbreak, and immunology.

Harvey, Barbara. *Living and Dying in England, 1100–1540: The Monastic Experience*. Oxford: Clarendon Press, 1993. A carefully researched account of what life was like in a medieval monastery. The portions on plague are short but vivid.

Hatcher, John. *The Black Death: A Personal History*. De Capo Press, 2009. A quirky book that is half history, half fiction—a brave attempt to "bring the period to life" that is carefully researched. Contains much interesting information about daily life in an English village affected by the plague.

———. *Plague, Population and the English Economy 1348–1530*. London: Macmillan, 1977. A slim volume that nonetheless thoroughly investigates why the English economy and population remained depressed for almost two centuries after the first outbreak of plague.

Herlihy, David. *The Black Death and the Transformation of the West*. Cambridge, MA: Harvard University Press, 1997. This book is in fact three lectures that were given by the renowned professor, edited and turned into book form after his death. Includes some fascinating details and offers original arguments about how, exactly, the plague helped the medieval world transform into the modern one.

Hilton, R.H. and T.H. Aston, eds. *The English Rising of 1381*. Cambridge: Cambridge University Press, 1984. A collection of articles that situates the uprising in context with the Black Death and several other political and social events, including the Jacquerie in France and uprisings in Florence, Italy.

Horrox, Rosemary. *The Black Death*. Manchester and New York: Manchester University Press, 1994. The standard edition of contemporary documents related to the Black Death, all in modern English translation. A goldmine of information, arranged both topically and chronologically with helpful notes.

Howard, Donald R. *Chaucer: His Life, His Works, His World*. New York: Ballantine Books, 1989. A bit dated, but still highly readable and comprehensive study of Chaucer and his milieu.

Kelly, John. *The Great Mortality: An Intimate History of the Black Death* (London, Harper Perennial, 2013). Intended for a popular audience; uses primary source materials as a starting point to imagine what life was like during the Black Death. Highly readable, if not always scrupulously accurate.

Kelly, Maria. *A History of the Black Death in In Ireland*. Stroud, UK: Tempus, 2001. A focused study on how the plague affected both Irish-Gaelic and Anglo-Irish society, with emphases on economics, politics, and religion.

Langer, Lawrence N. "Plague and the Russian Countryside: Monastic Estates in the Late Fourteenth and Early Fifteenth Centuries." *Canadian-American Slavic Studies* 10.3 (1976): 351–368. Explores how the plague transformed Russia and allowed monastic entities to acquire disproportionate land and power. Takes care to note how ruling powers in Moscow were not powerful enough to cope with the crisis caused by plague.

Meiss, Millard. *Painting in Florence and Siena after the Black Death: The Arts, Religion, and Society in the Mid-Fourteenth Century*. Princeton: Princeton University Press, 1979. The starting point for all current discussions of how the Tuscan artistic community responded to the plague. A bit dated, and some of his points have been disproven, but still worth a read.

Najemy, John M. *A History of Florence: 1200–1575* (Oxford: Blackwell, 2006). A masterful study of the jewel in the Tuscan crown. Explores how Florence's identity was shaped by its economics, family relationships, the tension between elites and the *popolo*, revolutions and uprisings, the papacy, and more.

Nohl, Johannes. *The Black Death: A Chronicle of the Plague*. Trans. C.H. Clarke. London: G. Allen & Unwin, 1926; repr. New York: Ballantine Books, 1960. Focuses on some of the more sensational responses to plague, including plague dance parties and hedonism in the face of death. Not quite as scholarly rigorous as it could be.

Ormrod, Mark and Phillip Lindley, eds. *The Black Death in England*. Stamford: Paul Watkins, 1996. Collection of articles by scholars on topics including the economic impact, effect on the Church in England, and government/politics.

Platt, Colin. *King Death: The Black Death and Its Aftermath in Late-Medieval England* (London: UCL Press, 1996). A survey of what life was like in a variety of professions in medieval England, including among the nobility, the clergy, villagers/townspeople, artists and artisans, etc. Includes some great black and white photos.

Rollo-Koster, Joëlle. *Avignon and Its Papacy, 1309–1417: Popes, Institutions, and Society* (New York and London: Rowman and Littlefield, 2015). A thoroughly researched study of the Avignon Papacy in the context of the medieval

Church, with significant attention devoted to how the plague impacted this highest ecclesiastical office.

Rosenwein, Barbara. *A Short History of the Middle Ages*. 3rd edition. Orchard Park, NY: Broadview Press, 2004. The best introduction to the medieval period currently available. Although designed as a textbook, still highly readable. Crammed full of illustrations, maps, family trees, and other visual aids that help bring the period to life.

Slack, Paul. *Plague: A Very Short Introduction*. Oxford: Oxford University Press, 2012. Part of the excellent "very short introduction" series from Oxford. Concise, thorough, and covering all the basics from plague's epidemiology, its historical impact during the three pandemics, and recent critical debate about whether *Yersinia pestis* was the real culprit.

Tangherlini, Timothy R. "Ships, Fogs, and Traveling Pairs: Plague Legend Migration in Scandinavia." *The Journal of American Folklore* 101. 400 (1988): 176–206. A fascinating examination of heretofore little-studied plague stories from Norway and Sweden. Notes the difference in plague folklore in Denmark as compared to the previously mentioned two other countries.

Wheelis, Mark. "Biological Warfare at the 1346 Siege of Caffa." *Emerging Infectious Diseases* 8.9 (2002): 971–975. Fascinating but short article about the supposed "first contact" between the medieval European world and the plague.

Williman, Daniel, ed. *The Black Death: The Impact of the Fourteenth Century Plague*. Binghamton, NY: Medieval and Renaissance Texts and Studies, 1982. A collection of seven different articles that were the products of an academic conference on plague. Various topics include plague in the Islamic world, plague in the countryside, specific impacts on art and literature, and religious eschatological responses. Interesting collection, if not terribly unified in terms of approach.

Ziegler, Phillip. *The Black Death*. New York: Harper and Row, 1969. Long considered the standard treatment of the Black Death; organized primarily by geography, but exploring a diverse range of thematic topics. A key text in the study of the plague.

Zguta, Russel. "The One-Day Votive Church: A Religious Response to the Black Death in Early Russia." *Slavic Review* 40.3 (1981): 423–432. While focused primarily on responses to plague that occurred during later outbreaks—and not the initial wave of the mid-fourteenth century—offers a fascinating window into a unique cultural/psychosocial response to plague.

IMAGE CREDITS

NOTES

NOTES

NOTES

NOTES

NOTES